RELUCTA
REFUG

The Story of Asylum in Britain

RELUCTANT REFUGE

The Story of Asylum in Britain

—

DR EDIE FRIEDMAN

AND

REVA KLEIN

FOREWORD BY

MAEVE SHERLOCK

former Chief Executive, Refugee Council

THE BRITISH LIBRARY

First published 2008 by
The British Library
96 Euston Road
London NW1 2DB

© 2008 Dr Edie Friedman and Reva Klein

British Library Cataloguing-in-Publication Data
A Catalogue record for this book is available
from The British Library

ISBN 978 0 7123 0887 8

Designed by Bob Elliott

Typeset at The Spartan Press Ltd,
Lymington, Hants

Printed by the MPG Books Group in the UK

To Anthony and Anna, to Brian, Jodie and Max,
and to the courage and tenacity of refugees, past and present.

CONTENTS

—

FOREWORD

During the General Election, in 2005, asylum and immigration routinely featured in the list of issues of most concern to the electorate. This may surprise some people since it arguably affects far fewer voters than topics such as education, health or tax. But it has always been controversial. Everyone in Britain has an opinion about asylum, though in my experience no more than one in ten of them knows what it means. Even those who have worked out that asylum seekers are just people who have applied to be recognised as refugees assume that most don't really need to be here.

The reality of refugee movements is an accumulation of personal stories played out against the backdrop of international conflict and persecution around the world. But in our media the stories only start on the day refugees step onto British soil. In film parlance, refugees have no 'backstory'. They are seen only as supplicants needing our help, while the story of what they fled and the courage they may have shown in escaping it are invisible. There is not even a reference to their past lives: no sense that today's refugees were yesterday simply mothers, brothers, children, doctors, teachers, builders, often ordinary people to whom extraordinary things happened.

Neither is there an appropriate sense of history or perspective on the issue. Many people who speak to me about refugees or asylum-seekers either assume that this is a new phenomenon, or they believe that earlier generations of refugees – Jews, Huguenots – were 'real' refugees while their modern-day counterparts are not.

This book begins to restore some of the context and history so sorely missing from this national debate. It begins with the family stories of the authors and then opens out to show us

some of the history, geography and politics that have underpinned refugee flight for so long.

The early chapters illustrate that, far from being a modern
phenomenon, people have come here for centuries fleeing
persecution. It also shows that the hostility sometimes dis-
played to those given sanctuary here is not new either. Some of
the quotations from newspapers of decades ago feel so familiar
in sentiment that it is a shock to realise they are not contemporary. The book goes on to chronicle some of the (as-
tonishingly many) changes that have been made to law and
practice in the UK and elsewhere in Europe to deter those
wanting to claim asylum from coming to Britain.

In this book Edie and Reva show us, time and again, how
great is the gap between myth and reality when it comes to
asylum. It also throws out a real challenge to a rich nation like
the UK to consider our attitudes to those who need protection
from persecution. This book should remind us to give thanks
for the Geneva Convention, and especially the Refugee Convention. There are not many international treaties that can
safely be said to have saved millions of lives, but the Refugee
Convention is one. I hope that once you have read this, you
will become one of the very many people who will stand up for
the right to asylum.

Maeve Sherlock
Chief Executive, The Refugee Council (2003–6)
November 2005

ACKNOWLEDGEMENTS

The authors are deeply indebted to Anthony Warshaw, formerly of the British Library, for commissioning this book, and to Lara Speicher and Joanna Macnamara, his successors, for aiding its delivery. We should also like to thank the Press Department at the Medical Foundation for the Care of Victims of Torture for their help in providing essential information, and Liz Hoar and Helen Johnson at the Refugee Council for their careful fact-checking. Dr Hermione Harris graciously shared her research and was a source of calm and good-natured guidance. The staff at Finsbury Park Homeless Project and the Bayswater Centre were enormously helpful in setting up interviews and smoothing the way for us and the University of East London and Refugee Action went beyond the call of duty to guide us through a morass of material. Those women and men who opened their hearts and memories in interview, some of them for the first time, always with difficulty, deserve particular gratitude. A number of people generously gave of their time to read various chapters and provided useful comments: Naomi Connelly, Jonathan Cox, Tim Finch, Jonathan Gorsky, Rachel Heilbron, Anthony Isaacs, Roberta Rosefield, Julie Taylor and Liza Schuster and Christine Beddoe. Special thanks to Karen Goodman and Judith Dennis for all their help in updating Chapter Six. We are especially grateful to Tony Kushner and Miranda Lewis for reading the entire manuscript and offering invaluable suggestions. Katarina Lester typed most of the manuscript; Chris Mohr edited it and Vivienne Kaye, John Shlackman and Maureen Fisher provided administrative support. Finally, we should like to thank our respective partners, Anthony and Brian, for their support, clear mindedness and infinite patience.

AUTHORS' INTRODUCTIONS

I am the grandchild of Jewish refugees from Russia who came to the United States in 1919 during a period of mass immigration from Eastern Europe. Between 1880 and 1920 over two million Jews came to the United States. Most of them, like my grandmother, disembarked at Ellis Island off the shores of New York City, where over 70 per cent of all Americans can trace their arrival on American soil.

I am not sure why my grandparents fled from Russia, whether it was to escape poverty or persecution or (in my grandfather's case) conscription. It could have been all three. They eventually arrived in Chicago by a circuitous route via Salonica in Greece. My grandfather was a professional violinist but his musical skills were not readily adaptable to his new country, burdened as it was by economic hardship. Entry into the music profession was only possible through membership of a musicians' union and union fees for this newly arrived, poverty-stricken violinist were out of the question. Employment at a factory provided the only possibility to earn money to pay the fees and sustain his young family. Ultimately his hands suffered as a result of working in the factory, the violin rotted in the cupboard of their tenement flat and, with it, the dreams of a lifetime. He never played the fiddle again. His story reflects the hopes and realities of millions of other refugees/economic migrants.

The distinction between those fleeing persecution and those escaping grinding poverty is often not clear cut, a point that is exploited by politicians to appeal to populist sentiment and by the media to whip up anti-immigration passion. The notion of the 'genuine' refugee is set against that of the 'bogus' asylum seeker or economic migrant.

It is not necessary to know any refugees to have passionate

views about them. The Institute for Public Policy Research conducted a survey in 2005 which revealed that most people in the United Kingdom have never met an asylum seeker or refugee. The press, however, has created the relationship for us all, complete with 'facts'. Asylum seekers and refugees are responsible for the shortages in housing and jobs, for longer NHS queues and the increase in crime and disorder. The equation becomes simple: they take more, we have less. Add to this the anxiety generated by the fear of terrorism and the linking of the words 'asylum seekers' and 'terrorism' and it is not difficult to see how attitudes towards asylum seekers have hardened. The government has done little to assuage people's anxieties as it seldom has anything positive to say about asylum seekers. When ministers do speak, their words are often couched in ambiguities. Thus the rhetoric from both press and government has coalesced to create a climate in which the far right can flourish, as seen by the British National Party's electoral success in national elections in 2006.

This book is published over a century after the introduction of the 1905 Aliens Act, the first significant legislation to curtail the number of immigrants and refugees coming to Britain. It is intended as a lay person's guide – an easily accessible overview of asylum and refugee issues – rather than as a contribution to the now substantial and rapidly expanding body of academic research on the subject. It also places these issues in their historical context in an attempt to disentangle some of the complexities that cloud our understanding of asylum seekers and refugees in Britain. In the process it sets out to challenge specific myths, attitudes and misconceptions about refugees in order to contribute to a more informed and rounded approach to current public policy debate.

In addition, the human realities of being an asylum seeker will hopefully be conveyed to readers of this book. While refugees' and asylum seekers' voices are generally absent from the debate, they are included here as an essential component for enhancing understanding of their lives, past and present.

Refugees are ordinary people to whom something extraordinary has happened.

Without acknowledging this basic fact, the discourse cannot be truly informed, open and balanced.

Edie Friedman, July 2007

The complex issue of refugees and asylum seekers has particular resonance for those of us who would not exist today had their parents or grandparents not managed to escape war and persecution by fleeing to other countries.

It certainly is *not* thanks to a humane asylum policy that I am sitting here today. My father, a Polish Jew from the Ukraine, escaped the fate of almost every other Jew in his village in 1942, including his mother and brother, who were shot in the forest by SS troops. He was one of the couple of thousand Jews improbably saved by Chiune Sugihara, the Japanese ambassador to Lithuania, at a time when no other country would accept Jews clamouring to escape Eastern Europe. Sugihara knew that awarding visas to the Jews who came knocking at the door of his embassy would mean the end of his career – and possibly worse. But he also knew, as he said in later interviews, that he wouldn't have been able to live with the blood of those Jews on his conscience if he had turned them away.

Thanks to Sugihara and his wife Yukiko, who encouraged him to help the desperate band of refugees on his doorstep, my father survived the war in the International Settlement in Japanese-occupied Shanghai, under the auspices of the International Committee of the Red Cross. He lived through seven long years of enormous privations, disease and threats of violence while his cousins, already in the American Midwest, tried pleading, then bribery and whatever other chicanery was at their disposal to get him a visa. Draconian US immigration quotas were loosened temporarily after the war through the Displaced Persons Act, which allowed approximately 400,000 refugees to enter. But quotas tightened again soon after. In fact, American asylum policy was far more humane towards eastern Europeans fleeing Communist regimes in the cold war years of the 1950s and 1960s than towards the survivors of the Second World War in its immediate aftermath. Still, all his cousins' blandishments finally paid off. Thanks to an Illinois congressman, my father was eventually awarded a visa in 1949 and soon after embarked on a long journey that would end with a new beginning in America.

His was only one story out of many millions who were caught up in a century of unprecedented brutality, upheaval and displacement. Today, just sixty-three years since the end of the Second World War, we find ourselves in the midst of a negative current of political and social positioning against refugees that has been slowly but inexorably gaining momentum for decades. Laws unprecedented in their restrictiveness have found their ways onto statute books across the western world, creating barriers, fortresses, impenetrable walls at borders and ports, in an attempt to keep out the desperate and vulnerable. The 1951 UN Convention Relating to the Status of Refugees is being condemned in some quarters as out of date. Ours has become a world where the notion of immigration controls has superseded that of humanitarian protection, where the word *refugee* itself is seen as an epithet and anachronism, where the veracity of asylum seekers' claims of persecution is being doubted as never before.

Before we become completely swept up in these tidal changes for evermore, we need to ask ourselves, as well as our political, community and religious leaders, some uncomfortable questions. Does the 1951 UN Convention on Refugees have any relevance today? If not, why not? Why have asylum seekers become the global scapegoats and pariahs of countries north and south, east and west? Will today's refugees have stories to tell of how they were treated with humanity and respect by the individuals, organisations and governments of countries to which they have gone for help? Or will they, instead, carry through their lives indelible echoes of the disdain, disbelief and dislike with which they were met? How much longer will governments of countries like the United States and Britain be able to congratulate themselves on upholding the human rights of those fleeing persecution or hunger, those 'huddled masses yearning to be free'?[1] And perhaps most important of all, if we are so distrustful of the outsider, what future is there for us – collectively or as individuals? If we can so easily turn our backs on those who are oppressed and desperate, what has become of our humanity?

Reva Klein, July 2007

NOTES

The title of our book, *Reluctant Refuge*, refers to the ambivalence which Britain has shown, on and off, to those seeking asylum over the centuries. It in no way seeks to diminish the humanitarianism that has characterised certain chapters in the long history of refugees coming to this country, both on a government level and on the part of individuals and institutions.

1   Words from Emma Lazarus' famous poem 'The New Colossus', written in 1883 and engraved on a plaque on the Statue of Liberty.

THE CONCEPT OF ASYLUM

There are few more contentious or complex issues facing the international community today than the movement of people from one part of the world to another. The nature of these movements is diverse but driven by two basic motives: migrants' pursuit of better economic prospects and asylum seekers' pursuit of freedom from persecution or the fear of it. The two groups represent the push and pull element of global migration: those who are *pushed* are driven out of their countries against their will by factors that impact negatively on their lives, such as war and civil unrest, while those who are *pulled* are being drawn to a different country where they hope to experience economic advantages.

The debates surrounding migration that rage in the developed world are triggered by a variety of factors: by domestic issues, such as the rise in unemployment or illegal immigration; by the release of new figures showing high numbers of migrants/asylum seekers; or by international crises such as the 'war on terror' in its various guises. When it comes to asylum, the discourse becomes particularly vexed, contradictory and confusing. For the past century, with a few notable exceptions, the concept and presence of asylum seekers has been the stuff of parliamentary wrangles, vilification in the press and media and virulent opposition from right-wing groups, standing in stark contrast to the official national narrative of Britain as a compassionate liberal democracy providing a sanctuary to the persecuted of the world.

Much of what typifies the UK's paradoxical stand on asylum can be seen in *Controlling Our Borders: Making Migration Work for Britain,* the government's five-year strategy for asylum and immigration presented to Parliament by the then Home Secretary Charles Clarke. Opening with a statement on its commitment to the moral duty to 'protect those genuinely fleeing death or persecution', it then sets out its plan to tighten borders and restrictions on who may enter the UK.[1] Its justification for doing so is stated clearly: since the late 1980s the asylum system has been abused to a significant extent by economic migrants posing as asylum seekers fleeing persecution. This trend is mainly attributed to migrants' belief that this gives them a better chance of staying in this country because of the judderingly slow and bureaucratic asylum process, coupled with notorious difficulties in deporting failed applicants. The reasons for migrants posing as asylum seekers are seen somewhat differently by Justice, the British section of the International Commission of Jurists. In its submission to the inquiry on new approaches to the asylum process by the House of Lords Select Committee on the European Union, it suggests that 'in the absence of viable, legal migration routes to EU countries, persons who are not refugees are seeking to enter countries of their choice through the asylum channel, it being often the only entrance effectively open to them.'[2] Either way, reform of the system, including the way immigration and asylum policy is framed, is necessary for a number of reasons, not least of which is to put an end to the criminalisation of large numbers of people. For reform to work for the benefit of UK citizens as well as for asylum seekers and migrants, it also needs to be conceptualised and implemented together with fellow EU member states.

While in the past anti-asylum sentiment and rhetoric were crude expressions of prejudice, whether in terms of religion, race, economic status or a combination of those factors, more recently they have focused on the disbelief in claims of persecution. This has not come out of the blue: the government's response to the numbers of people entering this country illegally, itself often a response to media reports, has been negative and punitive. Unsurprisingly this has led to the widespread belief that most asylum seekers must be 'bogus' because otherwise they would enter legally. The 2006 Parliamentary furore – sparked by the Home Office's admission that it had lost track of an unknown number of failed asylum seekers – has led to reforms designed to make the processing of asylum applications more efficient, i.e. to speed up decisions and more systematically administer 'removals' (deportations) of those who fail their appeals.

While the debate continues about whether this country is sinking under the weight of 'illegal asylum seekers' or whether it would be sunk were it not for these people coming and taking on low-paid jobs that no one else wants to do, it is clear the government must stem the flow of illegal trafficking in order to bring some semblance of coherence to the system, let alone moderate public opinion. Another, humanitarian, reason why people should not be forced into illegality to seek refuge from persecution is to curb the exploitation and abuse that traffickers perpetrate against these vulnerable people. Yet this too is complicated, as Michael Dummett points out: traffickers often supply the only escape route to people desperate to escape persecution when all other paths are blocked.[3]

Among theorists and non-theorists alike the asylum issue has given rise to a fundamental questioning of the state's obligation to accept these people into the country. While a humanitarian and human rights perspective such as Dummett's holds that states have a moral duty to give refuge to those who seek it, the law sees it somewhat differently. States are free of any legal obligation to accept asylum seekers. As de Visscher puts it: 'That which is called a right to asylum is nothing more than the facility of each state to offer it to those that request it.'[4] Although governments who reject the concept of the right to asylum wholesale risk losing their credibility as liberal democracies at home and abroad, they have other means of blocking the way to asylum seekers, as we are seeing in the UK and throughout the European Union. Michael Dummett argues for a different interpretation of the role of the state vis-à-vis asylum seekers, one which is based on humanitarian principles in the broadest sense, to replace the narrow boundaries set down in the 1951 UN Convention on Refugees, and which accepts that there are reasons apart from a well-founded fear of being persecuted that would impel individuals to leave their homes, such as the impossibility of living a decent life there.[5]

Recently there has been a tendency for the asylum question to be framed in such a way as to prioritise the rights of citizens over those who are not citizens, and to suggest that citizens' rights are at risk if they are made universal, i.e. if they are given to non-citizens. Particularist theorists argue that states have a duty to prioritise their own citizens, given the supposed limitation of resources and the presumed will of the people themselves to be prioritised over foreigners. Liza Schuster points to James Hathaway's exploration of the problem, which contextualises it by saying that 'the pursuit by states of their own well-being has been the greatest factor shaping the international legal response to refugees since World War Two'. Hathaway sees the purpose of asylum and current refugee law as being 'to govern disruptions of regulated international migration in accordance with the interests of states'[6] – rather than existing for the benefit of the refugees themselves. Humanitarian considerations, in other words, have been superseded by self-interest. Others, including Walzer, have shown how the issue of asylum has become 'a tough proving ground for theories of justice, sovereignty, citizenship or political obligation'.[7] For Liza Schuster, a 'radical – revolutionary – rethinking of the agenda' is called for to break out of the limited and limiting discourse that currently exists on asylum. 'The dreams of a world that is no longer divided into exclusionary and chauvinistic states are unlikely to come to fruition in the immediate future, but such dreams are evidence that it is at least possible to conceive of alternatives to a world of bounded states with sedentary populations.'[8]

The 'organised hypocrisy'[9] with which western states deal with asylum seekers reflects what Matthew Gibney calls 'a kind of schizophrenia' that has taken hold. 'Great importance is attached to the principle of asylum but enormous efforts are made to ensure that refugees (and those with less pressing claims) never reach the territory of the state where they could

receive its protection."[10] Gibney argues for governments to
repudiate the hypocrisy that has dictated policy towards asylum seekers and instead work towards a realistic humanitarian approach that will reshape the 'political space',[11] making it
more positive towards seeking asylum. He suggests a three-
pronged approach: reworking public opinion through campaigns and public policy statements involving all three of the
major political parties; co-operating internationally to equit-
ably share the resettlement needs of refugees; and attempting
to tackle the root causes of forced migration. This last point,
although ambitious and complex, would involve banning
small arms trade, setting up more liberal trade access to
western markets for producers in the developing world and
making carefully planned development aid available for specific purposes. While he concedes that 'real world constraints'
present challenges when developing more inclusive refugee
policies, he argues that 'by requiring that the governments of
liberal democracies take the moral claims of refugees and
asylum seekers more seriously, the humanitarian principle
might move these states closer to realising the values they
claim to live by now'.[12]

That a rethinking of asylum principles and policies is long
overdue is, say theorists, activists and politicians alike, beyond
question. What is less clear is in which direction this thinking
should be going and whose interests come first in these most
globalised of times.

NOTES

1 C. Clarke, *Controlling our Borders: Making Migration Work for Britain*
   (London, Stationery Office, 2005), p. 17.

2 JUSTICE House of Lords Select Committee on the European Union
   Sub-Committee F, Inquiry on New Approaches to the Asylum Process:
   JUSTICE's Response (2003). Available at www.justice.org.uk/images/
   pdfs/asylumnewapp.pdf (accessed 10 October 2007).

3 M. Dummett, *On Immigration and Refugees* (Routledge, Oxford, 2001) p. 29.

4 C. de Visscher, *Theories et Realities en Droit International Public* (1970), in L.

Schuster, *The Use and Abuse of Political Asylum in Britain and Germany* (Frank Cass, London, 2003), p. 223.

5 Dummett, *On Immigration and Refugees*, p. 32.

6 J. Hathaway, *A Reconsideration of the Underlying Premise of Refugee Law*, Harvard International Law Journal 31, 1 (1990), 129–83, quoted in Schuster, *Use and Abuse of Political Asylum*, p. 2.

7 M. Walzer, *Spheres of Justice: A Defence of Pluralism and Equality* (1983) in Schuster, *Use and Abuse of Political Asylum*, p. 2.

8 Schuster, *Use and Abuse of Political Asylum*, pp. 276–7.

9 S. D. Krasner, *Sovereignty: Organised Hypocrisy* (1999) in M. Gibney, *The Ethics and Politics of Asylum* (Cambridge University Press: Cambridge 2004), p. 2.

10 M. Gibney, *The Ethics and Politics of Asylum*, p. 2.

11 Ibid., p. 244.

12 Ibid., p. 260.

—

CHAPTER ONE

Refugees to Britain before the Second World War

LOOKING back at some of the major refugee groups who came to Britain through history, at their reasons for coming, at the political and social responses to their arrival and at their experiences of settlement, helps shed light on how we think about asylum today. What becomes clear through their discrete stories is that the prevailing climate of anti-asylum policies and attitude are part of a continuum. There is nothing substantially new about today's smear and fear campaigns in the press, the political debates in Parliament arguing humanitarian action on the one hand and national self-interest on the other, the discrimination being played out in the streets and the xenophobia that has permeated the minds of even those on the left.

This chapter looks at two of the major refugee communities that settled in England before the middle of the twentieth century. Far from comprehensive, it is nonetheless representative of the range of experience documented. Exploring their reasons for coming and theirexperiences of settlement helps illuminate how, despite enormous diversities of religion, ethnicity, culture and class, the refugee experience in Britain presents certain commonalities throughout time.

PROTESTANT REFUGEES: THE HUGUENOTS

The Protestants constituted the first mass migration to the British Isles since the Normans, arriving from the Low

Countries, France, Switzerland, Spain and Germany from the end of the sixteenth century. Unlike the Normans they came not to conquer but to escape the waves of religious hatred sweeping across the continent in the wake of the Reformation.

In France the persecution and butchery began in 1562 when Catholic forces massacred a congregation of twelve hundred Huguenots at Vassy, setting off a religious civil war between the two groups lasting eight years. Branded heretics by the Catholic authorities in their adoption of Calvinism, Lutheranism and other strands of Protestantism, Huguenots had no time to become complacent. The notorious St Bartholomew's Day Massacre on 24 August 1572 sparked off anti-Protestant riots in Lyon and Bordeaux that led to the butchering of around 20,000 Huguenots across the country.[1] Catholics all over Europe, including the Pope and the Spanish king, were jubilant. It was not until 1598 that the killing ended and Henry IV's Edict of Nantes allowed Huguenots freedom to worship and awarded them other civil liberties within the Catholic state. By then many thousands had fled to the British Isles and the New World.

Like many refugee communities today, the Protestants clustered in particular areas and kept to their national groupings but, in contrast to most today, they included people of high social rank. Many others came as highly skilled workers, renowned for their craftsmanship in silk-weaving, as well as tailoring, shoemaking, wood and metalwork, printing, glassblowing and other trades.[2] They founded the Bank of England, brought windmills to Sandwich and introduced plumbing into Londoners' homes.

A second mass exodus from France took place after the Edict of Nantes was revoked in 1685, effectively outlawing Protestantism and signalling yet another wave of violence against the Huguenots. Those seeking intellectual as well as religious freedom from the Catholic tyranny left in their thousands, hiding their children in beer barrels. In their flight, they were frequently terrorised and occasionally captured en route by Spanish pirates and French patrols.[3]

The England of Charles II welcomed them with assurances of citizenship and the poor were given handouts raised by a relief committee. Some of this largesse was politically motivated. Given the enmity between the two countries, any enemy of France was a friend of England. It was also an opportunity for the king to curry favour with the Protestant majority at home. The Great Plague epidemic of the 1660s had left England desperate to repopulate. Here were people eager to do just that and boost the nation's fortunes in the process.

By the early seventeenth century the initial warmth and welcome towards the persecuted had chilled. The attitude towards Protestants from across the Channel had undergone a sea change. Anti-foreigner sentiment was not new to Britain. In the fifteenth century Richard III had passed a law prohibiting foreign artisans from settling in England except when employed as servants to Englishmen.[4] At the beginning of the eighteenth century the Protestant Naturalisation Act was passed in Parliament, giving full citizenship rights to the Huguenots and other Protestant refugees. But there was an outcry from the trade companies (early versions of trade unions) which reflected British protectionism as much as anti-French sentiment at a time of intermittent wars with France.

While the church had great sympathy with the Huguenots' plight and the middle classes admired their business acumen and artisanship, the French themselves were met with verbal abuse from all quarters, including MPs and the press, and were even accused of starting the Fire of London in 1666. Terrible overcrowding, poor housing, high unemployment, rampant TB and other diseases demanded a scapegoat and the foreigners were easy bait, even though the enormous influx into London at that time was largely a result of people streaming in from the provinces rather than from across the Channel. But this social unrest, coupled with resentment at the Frenchmen and women's industriousness and ingenuity, led to anti-French riots throughout the 1670s and 1680s.

In 1709 another wave of Protestant refugees arrived: ten thousand 'Poor Palatines', Rhineland Germans, pitched tents in London suburbs, glad to be free of anti-Protestant persecution and a succession of devastating wars and hunger. Unlike their Huguenot predecessors, most were impoverished agricultural workers lacking the ambition, skills and craftsmanship that would help them get on their feet in a rapidly urbanising England. The General Naturalisation Act passed earlier that year on the strength of the Huguenots' successful economic and social integration gave all foreign Protestants the right to naturalisation for a shilling. But the peasant Germans were regarded less benignly than the Huguenots. The outcry against them grew louder until, three years later, the act was repealed. Jonathan Swift, the social satirist and author of *Gulliver's Travels*, reflected the xenophobic zeitgeist when he derided 'those who love a Dutchman, a Palatine or a Frenchman better than a Briton'.[5]

Prominent descendants of Huguenots

- Winston Churchill, prime minister during the Second World War
- no fewer than ten American presidents, George Washington and the Roosevelts among them
- Paul Revere, aka Rivoire, revolutionary American who warned his fellow freedom-fighters that 'the English are coming' on his midnight ride
- Elizabeth, wife of Samuel Pepys, whose father was a converted Huguenot
- Henry David Thoreau, poet and essayist
- Henry Wadsworth Longfellow, poet
- Davy Crockett, aka Croquet, American frontier folk hero, immortalised as 'king of the wild frontier' in a popular song
- Buffalo Bill Cody, famous cowboy
- Louis Comfort Tiffany, stained glass artist and jeweller
- the Courtaulds, the textile manufacturing family

JEWISH REFUGEES

Jews first settled in England in the wake of the Norman Conquest of 1066 at the invitation of William the Conqueror. These early settlers weren't refugees; they were immigrants. Most were poor tradesmen but some were moneylenders from Rouen who helped to develop the financial industry in this country, including international trade networks. In exchange for bankrolling King John in his bid to reclaim Normandy, partially funding the costs of taking Wales and, ironically, bowing to pressures to contribute funding for the third crusade, they enjoyed special privileges and protection conferred on them by the king.

But the good times were short lived. Over the next couple of centuries a succession of accusations against Jews of ritually murdering children led to mass murders and progressively restrictive laws against them. Crippling taxation, laws removing their basic rights of ownership and to money lending for interest followed and the crown confiscated their goods, bonds and property. In a decree that has sinister echoes of the Nazi regime some seven hundred years later, Edward I forced all Jews over the age of seven to wear a yellow patch of cloth to mark them out as Jews. In 1290 the remaining Jews were banished from England (historians dispute the numbers expelled from anywhere between 15,000[6] to a mere 3,000).[7]

Jews were not officially readmitted until Cromwell's ascension to power in the mid seventeenth century. As refugees from the wars of the counter-Reformation in Spain, Portugal and the Low Countries they were viewed with sympathy in anti-Catholic, Reformation England. In the 1640s there was a large-scale pogrom in the Ukraine, in which an estimated 100,000 Jews were murdered. The survivors who fled to England formed the beginnings of an Ashkenazi community, Jews from eastern and central Europe, who co-existed with the Sephardim Jews of Spanish and Portuguese origin.

They settled in Spitalfields in the East End of London and the surrounding area, entered into the financial trade and attracted a mixture of admiration and derision, the latter culminating in public outcries and acts of parliament to curb their numbers. Whereas the Huguenots, their predecessors in Spitalfields, eventually became totally integrated into British customs and practices, the Jews, because of their religious observances, tended to keep themselves to themselves and retained their distinctive identity up until the eighteenth century.

While the 1753 Naturalisation Act only permitted a small number of Jews to become naturalised citizens (previously they had been deterred from doing so by a requirement to take the Anglican sacrament)[8] a torrent of antisemitic and xenophobic sentiment was unleashed. Despite this, one commentator observed that 'there was probably no country in Europe in which the Jews received better treatment'.[9]

The nineteenth century saw small numbers of political refugees coming to England from the continent, mostly nationalists and socialists. Another Naturalisation Act in 1870 made the length of residency in this country its major condition; later, good character and knowledge of English were added. Among the many political refugees who unsuccessfully applied for naturalisation in 1874 on the grounds that he was of undesirable character was Karl Marx.[10]

During the 19th century some 60 million Europeans left mainland Europe, mainly for the New World. As well as the 1840 potato famine in Ireland, there were famines elsewhere in western and northern Europe alongside the tail end of the Napoleonic Wars, failed revolutions and religious persecution. The ports of the north of England and Scotland were magnets for the poor Irish in particular: by the early 1860s they represented a quarter of the population of Liverpool. It was against this backdrop of widespread unemployment, hunger and immigration from Ireland and other countries that an estimated 120,000 to 150,000 Russian and Polish Jews settled in Britain. A small number of them fled the pogroms and sweeping restrictions on their activities in eastern Europe between

1870 and the beginning of the First World War. Many more came to escape poverty.

NOTES

1 Robert Winder, *Bloody Foreigners: The Story of Immigration to Britain* (London, Little, Brown, 2004), p. 49 and Henry White, *The Massacre of St Bartholomew, preceded by a history of the religious wars in the reign of Charles IX, 1868.* http://historian.net/massacre-st-bartholomew-preceded-history-religious-wars-reign-charles-ix-henry-white.html.

2 Commission for Racial Equality, *Roots of the Future: Ethnic Diversity in the Making of Britain* (London, 1996), p. 13.

3 Winder, *Bloody Foreigners*, p. 49.

4 W. Cunningham, *Alien Immigrants to England* (New York, Augustus M. Kelley, 1969), p. 119.

5 *The Examiner*, No. 2, 28 December 1710 in *Prose Works of Swift*, H. David (ed.), vol. 6, p. 95.

6 Cunningham, *Alien Immigrants*, p. 70.

7 V. G. Kiernan, 'Britain's old and new' in C. Holmes (ed.), *Immigrants and Minorities in British Society* (London, George Allen and Unwin, 1978), p. 27.

8 Kiernan, 'Britain's old and new', p. 48.

9 C. Roth, *The Jews of England* (Oxford, Oxford University Press, 1941).

10 Kiernan, 'Britain's old and new', p. 50.

CHAPTER TWO

A Place of Refuge?

CASE STUDY: JEWISH REFUGEES AS A PARADIGM FOR THE REFUGEE EXPERIENCE

Their unclean habits, their wretched clothing and miserable food enable them to perpetuate existence upon a pittance . . . these immigrants have flooded the labour market with cheap labour to such an extent to reduce thousands of native workers to the verge of destitution . . . Surely our own people have the first claim upon us.[1]

LOOKING back at the popular press's descriptions of Jewish refugees in the 1880s, it is clear that little has changed in the intervening century in terms of language and tone.[2] In fact the history of Jewish migration to Britain offers numerous parallels with the refugee experience today, as well as echoing some of the vagaries of current government policies, social provision, public opinion and media coverage.

The years from 1880–1914 were a period of continuous persecution, harassment and economic deprivation for Jews in Eastern Europe. During this period over three million Jews left Russia, Poland and Romania to escape pogroms,[3] poverty and conscription into the Russian army, the latter sometimes lasting as long as twenty years. Britain's Jewish community grew from 60,000 in 1880 to about 300,000 in 1914.

The arrival of such large numbers of refugees was met with a less than rapturous welcome by the government, the trade unions, certain newspapers and, indeed, sections of the Jewish community itself. Moreover, their arrival was the catalyst for the formation of several anti-Semitic groups, including the

British Brothers League in 1900, in some ways a forerunner of the British Union of Fascists. To begin with the Trades Union Congress fomented this anti-immigration debate, passing a number of resolutions between 1892 and 1895 calling for strict anti-alien legislation.[4] Inevitably, a number of politicians were happy to jump on this bandwagon. The Conservative party made alien restriction a central plank of its party platform after the 1900 general election.[5]

Until the end of the nineteenth century, refugees from European political regimes were largely welcomed by successive governments and were not subject to immigration restraints. It was not until the large-scale immigration of Jews from Russia and Eastern Europe that the 1905 Aliens Act was passed, restricting the entry of 'undesirable and destitute immigrants' who were considered to be a charge on public funds or posed a risk to public health.[6]

This Act included a provision to deport immigrants and in its first four years 1,378 Jews were deported, many of whom had lived with their families in the UK for years. Some of these deportations were done with the approval of the Jewish community. In 1888 the then main Jewish communal organisation in Britain, the Board of Guardians, prided itself on having arranged and funded repatriation of thousands of Jewish families.[7] Far more numerous were those refugees who were given financial and housing assistance by institutions within the Jewish community created precisely to help the new arrivals. But the generosity shown by some in the Jewish community was somewhat tempered by pressures from more settled Jews for the 'newcomers' to give up some of their 'foreign ways'. In 1881 the main British Jewish newspaper, the *Jewish Chronicle*, stated

> If they intend to remain in England, if they wish to become members of our community, we have a right to demand that they will show signs of an earnest wish for a complete amalgamation with the aims and the feelings of their host.[8]

The 1905 Aliens Act was followed by two subsequent acts of

Parliament: the Aliens Restrictions Acts of 1914 and 1919, which further limited the entry of aliens and restricted the movement of those already here, 'adding a heavy dose of post-war xenophobia and anti-Bolshevism to what were already extreme measures'.[9] The anti-alienism expressed during this period by a number of politicians, trade unions, certain sections of the press (and some quarters of the Jewish community itself) was to resurface after the next major wave of Jewish refugees in 1933 and again during subsequent waves of other refugees to Britain in the late twentieth and early twenty-first century.

The Jewish refugees who came in 1933 did so as a direct result of Hitler's accession to power. Initially, the United Kingdom's policy was directed at not interfering in Germany's so-called internal affairs. This view was reinforced by the belief that the arrival of Jewish refugees would be at variance with Britain's economic interests. There was, nevertheless, concerted pressure from a number of Jewish organisations as well as MPs and some church groups to admit more Jewish refugees. In 1938 the annexation of Austria (the Anschluss), and the German pogroms of November 9–10 (Kristallnacht) put increased pressure on the Government to relax restrictions on refugees.[10] Between Kristallnacht and the start of the war, 40,000 Jewish refugees were granted temporary residency in Britain.[11]

The fact that Britain took in these Jewish refugees has an iconic importance for its self-definition today as a generous and welcoming nation to the downtrodden of the world. As shown by the anniversaries of the end of the Second World War, the emphasis has been on Britain's heroic role, not only in defeating the Nazis but also in providing a haven for Jewish refugees. As a result, there is a popular belief that Britain went to war in order to save the Jews, though there is no evidence to support this view. In fact, the reality was rather different: there was considerable antagonism towards the refugees from all sections of society, and especially from some trade unions and certain sections of the press. An editorial in the *Sunday Express* in 1938 stated:

> [But] just now there is a big influx of foreign Jews into Britain. They are over-running the country. They are trying to enter the medical profession in great numbers. They wish to practise as dentists. Worst of all, many of them are holding themselves out to the public as psychoanalysts. There is no intolerance in Britain today. And by keeping a close watch on the causes that feed the intolerance of the Jews in other European countries, we shall be able to continue to treat well those Jews who have made their homes among us.[12]

Expressions of overt anti-Semitism were heard from various quarters. The actress Joyce Grenfell remarked, 'There is something a bit uncosy about a non-Aryan refugee in one's kitchen.'[13] Resistance also came from trade and professional bodies. Jewish refugee doctors trying to come to Britain before the war, for instance, had a difficult time. With the exception of the Socialist Medical Association, prominent medical organisations such as the British Medical Association and the Medical Practitioners Union lobbied to ensure that these refugee doctors would not be allowed into Britain before the war as they would 'dilute our industry'. A scheme to bring in 500 Austrian doctors before war broke out was rejected. Historian Tony Kushner quotes the infamous comment made by Lord Dawson, President of the Royal College of Physicians, in 1933: 'The number of refugee doctors who could usefully be absorbed, or teach us anything, could be counted on the fingers of one hand.'[14]

Negative attitudes towards Jewish refugees were also found in the Foreign Office, in contrast to more humanitarian concerns expressed by the Home Office:

> Senior Home Office officials were overwhelmingly sympathetic towards Jews. In this respect they compare favourably with their counterparts in the Foreign Office. Certainly, hostility towards Jews contributed to the lassitude with which Foreign Office officials generally responded to proposals for

humanitarian aid to Jews and to the vigour with which they argued against giving such aid. [15]

General anti-Jewish prejudice was instrumental in formulating government policy:

> What we can say is that British stereotypes of Jews were significant in marking them out as members of a group that was difficult, even dangerous, to help. Such prejudices helped to cast the image of the Jewish refugee in a problematic mould and thus to strengthen support for policies of restriction.[16]

At the same time, many non-Jews were sympathetic to the refugees, as were some religious organisations such as the Quakers. The Attenboroughs (parents of film director Richard, now Lord Attenborough, and Sir David Attenborough, the natural historian and broadcaster) adopted two Jewish children who came on the Kindertransport (a Government-sponsored programme in 1938–9 to admit Jewish children from Germany and the German-occupied territories, though not their parents).

By the start of the war, about 80,000 Jewish refugees had come to Britain, including 10,000 unaccompanied children on the Kindertransport.[17] (The United States refused to instigate a similar scheme on the grounds that it was against the will of God to separate children from their parents). In addition, 20,000 women were allowed to enter the country as domestic servants.[18]

Asylum in the United Kingdom was dependent on guarantees that the Jewish community would provide for all of the refugees' needs. Unsurprisingly, such a financial undertaking could not be sustained and the Government was eventually forced into providing some assistance. Whilst there was a huge amount of work done by Jewish individuals and organisations to help the refugees, the Jewish establishment itself was at times reluctant to demand that greater numbers should be allowed into Britain:[19]

> since political action qua Jews was precisely what they'd relinquished in return for civil rights and might, they feared,

be taken both as a criticism of the British government and ingratitude, thereby generating domestic anti-Semitism.[20]

Nevertheless, many more Jewish individuals and organisations rallied to lobby the government to allow in more refugees and then worked assiduously to assist in their integration after their arrival.

As the situation of European Jewry deteriorated, the British government's behaviour did not alter fundamentally: 'The problem of what to do with the Jews took precedence over saving them.'[21] Thus Britain's overall response to the plight of Jews was characterised by 'caution and pragmatism sub-ordinating humanitarianism to Britain's self-interest'.[22] It was also felt that their very presence would encourage even more anti-Semitism.[23] This belies the national myth that Britain went to war to save the Jews.

After the war, Britain's policy towards Jewish refugees became more restrictive.[24] Over 600,000 work permits were given out to displaced persons from Europe, of which only a few thousand went to Jews. In a post-war Britain experiencing an acute labour shortage, Jews did not fit into the 'economic requirements' it demanded: they were neither considered good workers nor were they thought likely to assimilate into the British way of life. This view was similar to the official thinking before the war:

> The Jews were not a pressing problem so long as they re-mained in the Nazis' clutches. Jews would cause serious inter-national embarrassment only if they escaped and became refugees . . . Jewish refugees were expected to arouse hostility and states were reluctant to accept them as immigrants.[25]

Children were the main beneficiaries of the government's post-war policy towards Jewish refugees though, compared to the need, the response was inadequate. The Home Office devised a policy to allow 1,000 Jewish orphans into the country on a temporary basis, though only 732 met their strict criteria. The policy towards adults was even less generous. Under the Distressed Relatives Scheme, a paltry 1,200 Jews were allowed into the country. The United States, which had a more stringent approach to accepting Jewish refugees both before and during the war, made some amends after the war by allowing in 100,000 refugees. In assessing Britain's record towards Jewish refugees, 'The conclusion cannot be avoided. Escape to Britain was an experience for a lucky few. Exclusion was the fate of the majority.'[26] This is in spite of an opinion poll conducted in 1943 which showed that 78 per cent of the respondents were in favour of admitting endangered Jews.[27]

Even after the war, however, anti-Jewish feelings still surfaced, as illustrated by a little-known episode in Hampstead, in north-west London, where many German Jewish refugees had settled. Around 3,000 residents signed a petition in October 1945 demanding that 'aliens of Hampstead' should be repatriated in order to free up housing for returning servicemen and women:

> Despite the emerging details regarding the depths of Nazi racial barbarity, the plight of Jewish refugees in Britain was not followed by a wave of compassion and reparation. Against a backdrop of generalised sentiment in favour of repatriation, the Jewish refugee was often viewed not as a deserving recipient of sympathy, but as a parasitic interloper depriving Hampstead's indigenous citizens of scarce resources . . .[28]

The petition mirrored generalised anti-alien sentiment within Britain. *The Times* newspaper campaigned for the repatriation of 'aliens' as a necessary prerequisite for the reconstruction of Europe. The term referred not only to Jews but also to Czechs, Poles and even the Free French. Thus refugees were charged with a two-pronged responsibility. The first was to stop using 'our' resources as there were others whose claims was more deserving. The second was to 'go back to where they came from' in order to aid in the reconstruction of their former country. Both arguments resonate with contemporary anti-asylum rhetoric: that government resources should be prioritised for British citizens and that asylum seekers should be repatriated for the sake of their home countries' development.

This antipathy towards Jewish refugees was a forewarning of 'the even greater hostility which was to be faced by future generations of immigrants and asylum seekers'.[29] Press and politicians have created new 'facts': refugees are a problem, essentially parasitic on our society rather than contributing to it. They repeat the mantra that restricting the entry of refugees is a necessary prerequisite for the achievement of 'good race relations'.[30] Another common 'fact' or myth is that their claims are without substance. With press and politicians repeatedly reinforcing this notion, a false dichotomy of the so-called 'genuine' and 'bogus' refugee has entered the language. This distinction is used to discredit the legitimacy of a person's right to asylum:

> The genuine refugee of popular mentality hardly exists in the here and now, but is firmly, and of course safely, located in the past where numbers are no longer a problem and action irrelevant.[31]

> It is thus ironic that the Jews from Eastern Europe at the turn of the 20th century and those escaping from the Third Reich in the 1930s have now become part of the elite club of historically designated 'genuine refugees' – the latest members being the Ugandan Asians – whom 'we' were right to help in the past. No politician or commentator, aside from those in neo-fascist organisations, would dare now to say that either the Huguenots or the Jews were anything but deserving of asylum.[32]

In 2002 the *Daily Express* claimed: 'Most immigrants are not genuine asylum seekers. They are young single men who have deserted their families for money.'[33] This climate of disbelief recalls the response made by an official of the Foreign Office, Arminius Dew, in September 1944 to those he thought to be exaggerating the horrors of Nazi persecution: 'In my opinion a disproportionate amount of the time of the office is wasted with these wailing Jews,' and again, 'What is distressing is the apparent readiness of the new Colonial Secretary to take this Jewish Agency "sob stuff" at its face value.'[34]

In order to counter the arguments and allegations made

against refugees, refugee organisations have made efforts to highlight the contribution refugees make to our society. This was and still is a two-edged sword. On the one hand it is appropriate to draw people's attention to the enormous contribution refugees have made in the past. On the other, an impression can be created that gaining asylum in this country should depend on whether or not asylum seekers/refugees have anything they can offer us. Are those with less significant skills not worthy of the same protection?

Playing the 'numbers game' – playing down the number of asylum seekers and refugees who enter the United Kingdom – can have a further detrimental effect on the refugee community. Those supporting the refugees against the Hampstead petitioners argued that the numbers cited in the anti-alien petition were grossly exaggerated, but:

> whilst it was necessary to refute the false information given by the petitioners, this drive to play down the numbers of refugees, and by implication the influence they wield both within the district and nationally, had the unfortunate consequences of adding to the dehumanisation of the refugees' plight, which was lost in the cold set of easily quantifiable statistics.[35]

In addition to being labelled as undesirable by host communities and the government, refugees have also received some antagonism from their own people who, although already established here, still live under a cloud of insecurity. It is born of a fear that increased immigration, particularly of the poor and 'culturally different', will exacerbate racism against the established minority communities. Throughout the century the Jewish establishment thought it imperative that Jewish refugees should acculturate as quickly as possible and, as discussed in Chapter 1, in the 1880s even helped repatriate thousands of families back to Eastern Europe.[36] These ambivalent attitudes were more recently echoed in a 1998 survey conducted by the Institute of Public Policy Research, which found that 48 per cent of Asians interviewed believed there was too much Asian immigration into Britain.

One of the inevitable consequences of this ambivalence is pressure to give up certain aspects of one's culture in order to blend in with the dominant social group. Such anxieties are common to many refugees and immigrants, irrespective of where they come from or where they are going. Such a sentiment is vividly depicted by the journalist Yasmin Alibhai-Brown, herself a refugee from Idi Amin's Uganda, as she reflects on growing up in that country in the 1960s:

> I dressed in mock Victorian clothes and did not walk too close to relatives with 'bad' accents. Others changed their names. Balwinders became Babs. We taught ourselves to forget how to eat rice with our hands and grappled foolishly with chicken legs as they flew off our forks. How Peter Sellers laughed. Thus we became adept at chiselling off any bits that might cause offence, trigger off painful rejections. But they came anyway. To add insult, the more we tried to belong the less we were respected.[37]

The black peer, Ros Howells, makes a similar point about growing up in the Caribbean:

> England was certainly the only place to come . . . It's like going to finishing school really . . . We didn't see England as a separate entity. For example, in my own convent school we spent a lot of time knitting little bits of wool for people during the war, you know the poor . . . We didn't see there was a difference between Grenada and England. 'There will always be an England and England shall be free' used to be one of our school songs . . . Empire Day was big in Grenada.[38]

Not all similarities between refugee experiences past and present are negative. Both in the early 1900s and today many refugees have shown striking resilience in their fight against anti-immigrant/asylum legislation as well as in their wide range of cultural expression. The East End of London was home to a diverse artistic community, from the Yiddish theatre to avant-garde painters (Mark Gertler, David Bomberg), poets (Isaac Rosenberg) and playwrights (Bernard Kops, Harold Pinter, Arnold Wesker). Today, refugees from over one hundred countries who now call Britain their home have organised hundreds of groups to cater for the needs of their respective communities and campaign for fairer asylum legislation. Those who are allowed to work are found in a wide array of skilled and unskilled jobs as well as teaching, law and medicine. Cultural expression is extensive and varied, ranging from the Iranian comedienne Shappi Khorsandi to the writer and Nobel Prize Winner Wole Soyinka.

One area of improvement for refugees today is in the attention paid to their psychological needs. It provides a stark contrast with previous generations of refugees, most notably Holocaust survivors, who were discouraged from talking about their horrific experiences. Although recently more have been telling their stories, it was not until the 50th anniversary of the liberation of Auschwitz in 1995 that many Jewish survivors here felt they had 'permission' to speak publicly about what had happened. A therapy centre for Holocaust survivors and their families was not established until 1990. In contrast, refugees today are encouraged to talk about their experiences as soon as they feel able. Post-traumatic stress disorder is now a well-recognised phenomenon and treatment centres such as the Medical Foundation for the Care of Victims of Torture have been set up, although these facilities tend to be under-resourced.[39]

There are also much better opportunities available for refugee doctors today. The antipathy shown by the medical establishment to Jewish refugee doctors in the 1930s has been replaced by a desire to ensure that their skills will not be lost. A great deal of work has gone into programmes to help today's refugee doctors to re-qualify, much of it spearheaded by the British Medical Association with financial support from the government.

These advances are not reflected, however, in the treatment that unaccompanied refugee children receive. As discussed in detail in Chapter 6, their predicament represents a failure to deal either compassionately or effectively with the situation.

Britain's image of itself, today as well as at the end of the

nineteenth century, has been that of a country with a proud
tradition of accepting those seeking sanctuary. Indeed, it forms
part of our national identity. But neither in the experiences
of Jewish refugees in the late nineteenth and early twentieth
century nor of those fleeing from Nazi-occupied Europe does
this national myth entirely stand up. Rather, we are left with a
picture of an ambivalent government that on the one hand
proclaims its humanitarian commitments and on the other
bows to populist opinion, reinforced by the inflammatory
rhetoric of certain sections of the press and trade unions:

> The reality is that, since 1905, the most 'generous' moments of
> British refugee policy have been the result of guilt, economic
> self-interest and international power politics, rather than of
> notions of 'natural justice' per se.[40]

It is assumed by some that Britain has 'done its bit' and can
leave it to other countries to take in refugees, and that this
country's compassion as well as its ability to cope with more
refugees has been exhausted. However, in understanding the
past and planning for the future, a balanced view of British
history is a necessary prerequisite for building a diverse and
inclusive society. Unrealistic perceptions of our historical
altruism cannot absolve us from our responsibilities towards
refugees and asylum seekers today.

NOTES

1 *Manchester City News*, 12 May 1888.

2 Roy Greenslade, *Seeking Scapegoats – The Coverage of Asylum in the UK Press*
(London, IPPR, 2005). 'But also important differences: the tone has become
more hysterical, the repetitious nature of the stories is more prevalent, and
the power of newspapers to set the agenda – both for other media and within
the political arena – is more potent, in spite of their declining sales.', p. 83.

3 'Pogrom' usually refers to an officially sanctioned, organised massacre of
Jews, primarily in Russia.

4 Robert Winder, *Bloody Foreigners: The Story of Immigration to Britain*,
(London, Little, Brown 2004), p. 197.

5   Tony Kushner and Katherine Knox, *Refugees in an Age of Genocide* (London, Frank Cass, 1999), p. 25.

6   One of the champions of the aliens' cause was the young Winston Churchill, who in 1904 in a letter to *The Times* stated that there was no good reason for Britain to give up 'the old tolerant and generous practice of free entry and asylum to which this country has so long adhered and from which it has so greatly gained.' As quoted in Winder, *Bloody Foreigners*, p. 198.

7   Anne Karpf, *The War After* (London, Minerva, 1996), p. 174.

8   As quoted by Winder, *Bloody Foreigners*, p. 178.

9   Kushner and Knox, *Refugees*, p. 74. Jews were not the only group who were the subject of the prevailing anti-alien sentiment. The Chinese community and, of course, the German community were also targeted.

10 Literally 'The Night of Broken Glass', anti-Semitic riots in which Jews were physically attacked and many synagogues destroyed.

11 Ibid., p. 9. Britain, like other western European countries such as France, Netherlands and Belgium was determined to offer primarily temporary, not permanent, refuge. This is in contrast to the United States, which though it also took a paltry number of refugees, saw itself as a country of 'permanent integration'.

12 *Sunday Express*, June 1938.

13 Anne Karpf, *The War After*, p. 178.

14 Tony Kushner in A. J. Sherman, *Island Refuge: Britain and the Refugees from the Third Reich* (London, Frank Cass, 1973), p. 83.

15 Louise London, *Whitehall and the Jews 1933–1948, British Immigration Policy and the Holocaust* (Cambridge, Cambridge University Press, 2000), p. 278.

16 Ibid., p. 277.

17 Ibid., p.12. At the start of the Second World War there were over 78,000 refugees in the UK, of whom some 70,000 were Jewish (excluding accompanied children). The number of Jews who were not allowed to come to Britain was ten times that.

18 Kushner and Knox, *Refugees in an Age of Genocide*, p. 157.

19 Mixed attitudes to new immigrants are not uncommon amongst established immigrants. A YouGov survey for the Commission for Racial Equality (June 2004) found that of the non-white people interviewed, 35 per cent had either a fairly low or very low opinion of people seeking asylum in Britain today. www.yougov.com/archives/pdf/RCF040101001_1.pdf. Other research which highlights this ambivalence is found in the IPPR 2005 Survey (see Chapter 7).

20 Karpf, *The War After*, p. 185.

21 Ibid., p. 2.

22 Ironically, post-war Britain (like the United States) became a haven for Nazi collaborators and war criminals. David Cesarani, *Justice Delayed*, cited in Karpf, *The War After*, p. 198.

23 London, *Whitehall and the Jews*, p. 12.

24 Ibid., p. 198. In the period 1945–50, 200,000 refugees, immigrant workers and displaced persons were admitted to Britain. Only around 1,200 were Jews, whereas over 10,000 Latvians were admitted.

25 Ibid., p. 282.

26 Ibid., p. 15.

27 Ibid., p. 15.

28 Graham D. Macklin, *A quite natural and moderate defensive feeling? The 1945 Hampstead 'anti-alien' petition, Patterns of Prejudice*, vol. 37, no. 3 (2003), p. 298.

29 Ibid., p. 299.

30 This theme was prominent in speeches made by the then Conservative leader Michael Howard during the 2005 general election campaign.

31 Tony Kushner, 'Meaning nothing but good: Ethics, history and asylum-seeker phobia in Britain', *Patterns of Prejudice*, vol. 37, no. 3 (2003), p. 266.

32 Ibid., p. 267.

33 *Daily Express*, 15 May 2002.

34 Quoted in *The Listener*, 16 September 1982 and by Max Hastings, *Guardian*, 11 March 2004.

35 Graham D. Macklin, 'A quite natural and moderate defensive feeling', p. 287.

36 Karpf, *The War After*, pp. 173–5.

37 Yasmin Alibhai-Brown, Introduction, *Who Do We Think We Are? Imagining the New Britain*, (London, Penguin 2000), p. 7.

38 Ibid., p. 92.

39 The Medical Foundation for the Care of Victims of Torture was established in 1985 under the auspices of the Medical Group of Amnesty International. Its focus is providing survivors of torture in the United Kingdom with medical treatment, practical assistance and psychotherapeutic support, documenting evidence of torture, providing training for health professionals working with torture survivors, educating the public and decision-makers about torture and its consequences and ensuring that Britain honours its international obligations towards survivors of torture, asylum seekers and refugees.

40 Kushner and Knox, *Refugees in An Age of Genocide*, (London, Frank Cass, 1999), p. 399.

CHAPTER THREE

Refugees to Britain since the Second World War:
Ugandan Asians, Somalis and Roma

THE earth-shattering events of the Second World War, after which an estimated 40 million Europeans were made refugees, took years to resolve. One small glimpse into the complexities of the situation can be gleaned from the fact that when the Allies attempted to repatriate more than six million displaced people to their home countries in 1945, between one and a half and two million refused. Many made their way to North America. Some 85,000 Ukrainians, Yugoslavs, Estonians, Latvians and Lithuanians came to Britain under government resettlement schemes run between 1946 and 1950.

The end of the war, of course, was not the end of the story of refugees in twentieth-century Europe. The consequent carving up of Europe between the Soviets and the Allies led to the upheavals of the Cold War and the forced migration of thousands from political repression and persecution. The unlamented passing of that protracted enmity has given rise to smaller, regional conflicts in Europe. And around the globe regional wars and conflicts have erupted since the cataclysmic effects of the Second World War. These events have cast millions of people far away from their homes, their families and everything they have known.

This chapter looks at three significant refugee groups who have come to Britain in the last thirty years. It includes individual's personal stories to help make vivid the problems they faced both before they left and after they arrived here and concludes with a brief account of other national/ethnic groups of refugees that have made their way to the UK over the past sixty years. Though by no means comprehensive, these examples offer some insight into the reasons they came here and what happened to them once they settled.

UGANDAN ASIANS: Melba's Story

Melba Ashworth, née Pereira, came to England aged thirteen with three of her nine siblings when Idi Amin expelled the Ugandan Asians in 1972.

> We thought the expulsion would never happen, but there were terrible incidents leading up to it. African soldiers would sometimes kill some Asian children on their way to school. We'd find their bodies along the way. I saw the Asian mayor of Masaka, our town, being battered to death by government troops. Then, one day, soldiers came to our house and accused my father of abusing one of them. My father was a well-known, respected member of the community and our family was accepted by the Africans. But these soldiers forced him onto his knees to beg for his life or they said they would imprison him. I went up to one of them and lashed out and screamed and kicked him. I'll never forget that image of my father on his knees. Soon after that, my father cleared the house because it was obvious we couldn't stay. He was a broken man. He had literally built this house and all his children had been born there. Uganda had been a safe place in my childhood until then and suddenly, it became a place of fear and unease.
>
> When I came to England, I was fostered by a Jewish family in Lewes, Sussex. I was Catholic; my family was originally from Goa, but I became very close to this family. The mother, Sonia, was the only person I could speak to. My own mother had died the year before and Sonia became like a mum to me.
>
> I had come from a small town with lots of different races and cultures in the school. In Lewes, I was the only 'coloured' in a sea of white. I'd never experienced racism before till someone at school called me 'blackie'.

I still can't face the idea of going back to Uganda. The memories of the expulsion are so painful.

Background

Small numbers of Asian traders had lived in east Africa since the 1400s. In the 1880s the colonial British transplanted tens of thousands of Indians – Muslims, Sikhs and Hindus – to the British protectorate for the purpose of building the Ugandan Railway. Over 31,000 labourers were put to work on the project, which took six years to complete, cost nearly 2,500 lives and became the cornerstone of Uganda's subsequent prosperity, crucial for the burgeoning cotton, coffee and sugar industries.

At the same time the British set about demarcating the boundaries of Uganda along purely arbitrary lines, ignoring existing ethnic and political demographics. The haphazard nature of these divisions unleashed tribal discord and unrest, setting the tone for the cataclysmic events of 70 years later.[1]

With the Asians in control of 80 per cent of the commerce, three-quarters of all industry and the overwhelming majority of the coffee, tea, tobacco, sugar and cotton estates, Africans' animosity was tremendous.[2] Anti-Asian rioting broke out regularly from 1945. After independence, President Milton Obote introduced restrictions on Asian business and financial activities. In August 1972 his successor, Idi Amin, went much further, ordering all 60,000 Asians to leave Uganda within 90 days. Violent attacks against Asians, including rape, torture and murder, were reported around the country in the wake of the ultimatum. By the November 1972 deadline most had left Uganda. Around 5,000 went to Canada, while others sought asylum in Malaysia and the US, or fled to their ancestral lands of India and Pakistan. The majority, around 250,000, came to this country as British passport-holders.[3]

While Britain, along with the rest of the world, expressed outrage at Amin's brutal treatment of the Asians, the government was unwilling to honour its responsibilities. Following

the post-war upturn in black and Asian immigration from
Commonwealth countries, race and immigration had become
highly politicised. Legislation introduced in 1962 had already
limited immigration of black and ethnic minority British
citizens from the Commonwealth. In 1968 MP Enoch Powell
made his infamous 'rivers of blood' speech warning of the
devastation that would befall Britain if more immigrants from
the Commonwealth were allowed to enter. This anticipated
large numbers of Kenyan Asians fleeing to Britain in response
to Kenyatta's anti-Asian Africanisation programme. In that
year the Commonwealth and Immigrants Act set a quota of
1,500 immigrants a year in response to anti-immigration
fever. In 1971 the Immigration Act effectively ended black
and Asian immigration by restricting rights to British residency for Commonwealth citizens. With anti-immigration
views expressed at all levels of British society and in the
press, Edward Heath's Conservative government feared that
the arrival of the Ugandan Asians would further inflame an
already inflammable situation. According to Cabinet papers
released in 2003 under the 30-year rule the government considered resettling the refugees on a far-flung island as an
alternative to bringing them to Britain. Among the less than
compelling possibilities considered were the Pacific Solomon
Islands and the Falklands.[4]

. . . *with only the clothes on their backs*

But come here they did, arriving with virtually nothing;
Amin's restrictions limited them to whatever they could carry
and a maximum of £50. To oversee their immediate needs the
Home Office set up the Uganda Resettlement Board, which
was essentially run by charities and voluntary organisations.
Emergency reception camps were rigged up at military bases in
the Home Counties and a national fundraising campaign was
launched to provide the refugees with basic supplies. In addition, several thousand people offered them shelter.

Once here, the refugees were warned against moving into
'red spot' areas highlighted on maps. These were towns and

cities with already high concentrations of Asians, including those from East Africa. Anticipating large numbers of refugees because of its well-established Asian community, Leicester City Council went so far as to place an advertisement in the Ugandan *Argus* entreating Asians 'in your own interests and those of your family' not to come to Leicester because of the lack of houses, jobs and school places in the city.[5] Nevertheless, nearly a quarter of the refugees sidestepped the camps to settle in the red areas. The 40 per cent who spent some time in a camp before finding housing for themselves moved into those cities and towns where the Ugandan Resettlement Board (URB) had tried to prevent them from settling.

Relying on the community's own entrepreneurial abilities instead, the Government failed to provide specially designed retraining or re-qualifying programmes; however, they were allowed the same entitlements as other citizens.[6] Similarly, no specific facilities were provided for those of retirement age, though benefits were available. One year on, the URB found widespread poverty and poor housing conditions among the refugees. The worst affected were those who had been dispersed into the 'green areas' (as opposed to those centres with a settled Asian population) where they suffered isolation and unemployment. Ten years later, a very different picture emerged: the refugees had achieved higher formal qualifications than either their Indian or white British counterparts and had also improved their socio-economic standing more quickly than either of the two groups. Many managed to establish small businesses through self-help, community-based development programmes.[7]

According to most socio-economic indicators, British Asian citizens of originally Indian descent are among the highest achievers in this country today. In wealth terms alone, 10 per cent of the 2003 Asian Rich List, which catalogues the 300 wealthiest Asians in Britain with a combined wealth of £8.9 billion, came from Uganda and Kenya. Leicester, the town that implored them to stay away 33 years ago, attributes 30,000 jobs in the city to the development of businesses by Ugandan

Asian entrepreneurs, a majority of them Hindu, with smaller numbers of Muslims and Sikhs.[8] A proportion of the nearly 30 per cent of Asian doctors working in the NHS are former refugees from Uganda or their descendants. Around 65 per cent of British citizens of Indian descent have an annual income of more than £30,000 and earn an average of £460 a week, in contrast to the average white adult's weekly income of £334.

Ugandan Asians join others of Indian descent in achieving extremely high academic standards in the British education system. More Indians in this country attain degrees – 39 per cent – than the total average of all ethnic categories, including whites. In the GCSE results of 2003, 65.2 per cent of Indian students achieved five or more A* to C grades, compared to nearly 75 per cent of the highest achieving ethnic group, students of Chinese origin. Only just over half of white students reach these grades.[9]

A group of businesspeople have set up the British-Asian Uganda Trust, which raises money for British charities. Chair of the Trust, multi-millionaire Manubhai Madhvani, may not be representative of Ugandan refugees. But he spoke for many Ugandan Asians when he told a reporter a few years ago, 'We came here 25 years ago full of anxiety in an unknown land. The British people extended a welcoming hand, enabling us to make this country our home. Very few people tend to say thank you. We intend to be different.'

SOMALIS: Ahmed's Story

Ahmed was driven out of Mogadishu, Somalia by militia activity in 1999. He came to Britain alone, as an unaccompanied minor.

> I travelled on the plane with my fixer . . . [who] came with me on a bus to central London and then took me to a phone box, where he phoned some family friends . . . He told them I was here and they should come and collect me. Then he just left

me there, in the phone box. I was very nervous. I didn't know what would happen to me. I waited for some time, then someone did come and took me to their house . . .

The mother was nice to me, but the children – they had been here a long time and they didn't like me. I was from Africa; everything about me was different. They were abusive and said very abusive things to me.

I lived with the family for one year but couldn't get on with them and was very unhappy. It was very difficult. The family would talk to each other and laugh but I was separate and didn't understand any of them . . .

My other problem was at school. I had been to secondary school [in Somalia] but I had a language problem. I sat in the class but there was a lot I didn't understand.

I miss my family a lot. I don't know how to contact them. If I had money, I would go. I hope eventually to find them . . . I should have stayed with them whatever was happening. Sending your child away is a disastrous idea . . . There are social services but it is full of empty promises. I got to see social workers . . . [but] . . . I am always dealing with different people who don't know me or anything about me. Life is very lonely.[10]

Background

Like so many countries in the post-colonial world, Somalia has suffered decades of strife, chaos and insecurity since gaining independence in 1960 from Britain and Italy. Its last general election, held in October 2004, had to take place in Kenya because Mogadishu, the Somali capital, was considered too dangerous. For similar reasons, the new government will not move to the capital: not surprising in a country called one of the most dangerous in the world by the UK-based Control Risks Group. The reasons for Somalia's deadly status are twofold. First, its lack of a stable central government for over ten years has led to widespread lawlessness and anarchy. Second, the emergence of a 'jihadi' group with al-Qaida connections, according to the Brussels-based International Crisis Group, together with the discovery of a network of 'terrorist training camps' there, highlighted in a 2005 UN report, has put Somalia on the map as a potential international powder keg.[11]

This is all a far cry from the traditional pastoral existence that Somalis have enjoyed for centuries. Mainly Sunni Muslims, they are descended from an ancient, mainly Arabian people. But years of devastating conflict have to some extent disrupted traditional ways of life and resulted in nearly half a million Somalis living as refugees either in neighbouring Kenya, Ethiopia, Djibouti or further afield. Some traditions have stuck, though. While Somali women and girls have greater educational, employment and travel opportunities than many other women in the region, Somali culture remains deeply patriarchal. The grimmest testament to that is the fact that an estimated 98 per cent of all Somali girls aged eight to ten are subjected to genital mutilation.

Somalia's instability predates its independence by seven decades. Following the opening of the Suez Canal at the end of the nineteenth century, Somalia was carved up by the British, French, Italians and, in the Ogaden region, the Ethiopians. In the Second World War the British won Italian Somalia and the Ogaden, bringing three-quarters of the country under their administration. After the former Italian Somalia and British Somaliland were fused together in 1960 to form an independent Somali Republic, progressive factionalism between clans spawned a large number of political parties and a succession of weak governments. At the same time a current of nationalistic Pan-Somalism led to armed conflicts with neighbouring Kenya and Ethiopia.

In 1969 a Soviet-backed coup led by Siyaad Barre resulted in a new socialist regime, ushering in an era of stability and progress. The aim was to build up an infrastructure, and to develop health, education and the rights of women and minorities. A written language was introduced, boosting literacy fivefold in under two decades. However, increasing levels of corruption, repression and human rights abuses perpetrated by the government spawned several opposition movements.

Civil war from the mid 1980s to 1991 culminated in Barre's overthrow. The country descended into mayhem and destruction, driven by local warlords and clan rivalries. An independent Somaliland Republic was declared in the north, and the south fragmented into two hostile entities. The violence brought disease and famine on a catastrophic scale: in a single year, one half of all children under the age of five died, along with hundreds of thousands of adults. Nearly half of all Somalis either fled to neighbouring countries for asylum or became internally displaced.

UN intervention and humanitarian aid from 1992 to 1995 was sabotaged by the local militias. Throughout the rest of the decade the warlords and government militias undermined all peace initiatives. Between 1989 and 2004 an estimated 400,000 Somalis were killed. The loss of one million more lives is attributed to the famine which mainly resulted from the war. Vast numbers fled their homes but remained in the region, mainly in Kenya, Yemen and Ethiopia. Over 429,000 Somali refugees are scattered around the world, making them the fifth largest group of refugees globally. Fighting still continues between clans in scattered pockets across the country. Only the northern territory, now the independent republic of Somaliland, is relatively peaceful and has received nearly 750,000 returnees who had fled during the worst of the conflict. The republic receives no official aid because it does not have international recognition.

Because of Britain's colonial history, there has been a Somalian community in this country since the nineteenth century. Somali men served as sailors on British ships during the First World War and later as merchant seamen, settling in dockland districts of London, Liverpool, Cardiff and elsewhere. These first groups were self-contained, seeing themselves as temporary residents. Many lived an isolated existence – living, working and retiring in this country. It was not until the 1950s that women joined their husbands, some of whom were working in the regenerating industries of post-war Britain. Small communities grew up in east London as well as in

Sheffield and Manchester, mainly originating from clans in northern Somalia. With the downsizing of the merchant navy and the recession of the 1970s many more found themselves on the dole and later on retired with minimal social and financial support.

Flight to Britain

The first group of Somali refugees (mainly women and children) fled during the armed conflicts of the 1980s, going to neighbouring Kenya or the Arabian Gulf states; others went further afield, to the United States, Germany, Scandinavia and Britain. A fresh wave arrived in the UK after the fall of Barre's government in 1991, so that today Britain hosts the largest Somali community in the world outside Somalia itself. Since 2000 there has been a steady increase in the numbers of people refused asylum in favour of short-term temporary protection provisions. In 2003 fewer than 50 per cent of applicants from Somalia were given leave to remain in the UK, in stark contrast to 1991–6, when 88 per cent were granted Exceptional Leave to Remain.* In 2004 Britain returned a hundred Somalis to what was acknowledged to be a dangerous and volatile country. However, Somalis also win a higher proportion of appeals against Home Office decisions than other groups. Where in 2003, 38 per cent of all Somali appeals were granted, only 26 per cent were granted to all other Africans and 19 per cent to asylum appeals overall. In the previous year 35 per cent of Somali appeals were allowed as opposed to an overall average of 22 per cent.

Large numbers of Somalis came in the late 1990s to join family members through the government's family reunion scheme. In 2002 10,000 Somalis – refugees and dependents of family members already settled here – were granted settlement, which means they are given leave to remain in the UK

---

*Until 1998 ELR was initially given for one year followed by six years, after which an asylum seeker could apply for Indefinite Leave to Remain (ILR). People granted ELR have more restricted entitlements than those who achieve refugee status.

indefinitely. Of the increasing number of Somalis whose asylum applications are turned down by the Home Office, very few are deported or return voluntarily, which means that substantial numbers are living here excluded from entitlement to benefits or rights to employment.

Overall, it is impossible to put a figure on how many Somalis actually reside in the UK or to determine the age profile, because of their low participation in the UK national census.* Estimates range from 60,000 to 250,000. A study in 1999 estimated that nearly 90 per cent of Somalis were unemployed and many had never had a job in this country. A 2002 study of two hundred Somalis, half of whom were refugees who had come within the last ten years, found that many had arrived with high educational and professional qualifications. Yet most were blocked from comparable employment in the UK either for reasons of asylum law or training requirements. Some Somalis have managed to draw on their entrepreneurial skills to set up businesses or work in refugee community organisations. The vast majority, however, suffer poverty and social exclusion.

Somali children appear to do poorly in school, but this depends on the age they were when they arrived here. Many have literacy problems in their own language, which puts them at a disadvantage when acquiring a second language. Others will have been traumatised by their experiences. Schools, especially in areas to which families have been dispersed, often lack the resources to provide additional language teaching or appropriate emotional support. For traditionalists, there may also be cultural barriers to education, such as opposition to mixed secondary education.

*The Somali disinclination to give personal details to the government census seems to be shared by a great many. The 2001 census results were missing several million people, particularly young men. The head of census analysis at the Office of National Statistics points to two factors that have led to this enormous shortfall in the census: first, the significance of the census was poorly or inadequately explained to 'some minority groups' and, second, many people in high density housing simply did not receive forms.

Somali culture and experience is distinct both from other black and from other African communities, and tensions exist. While, for some young people, their otherness can be a source of strength and support, there are those for whom it is a heavy burden to shoulder. Stuck betwixt and between generations and cultures, Somali youth can suffer the isolation and listlessness of the previous generation of unemployed, uneducated and impoverished sailors. As the report to the 2003 Somali Council meeting in London put it, 'Somali young people do not have a role model that they can imitate in every aspect of their lives. This community is very new to this society and up till now there are no successful stories that we could tell the young people.' This is now changing. Today's success stories include Ragi Omar, BBC TV journalist, Iman, supermodel and actress, and Warris, former supermodel, now UN Population Fund's goodwill ambassador for the Elimination of Female Genital Mutilation.[11]

(The above section on Somalis is based largely on Hermione Harris, *The Somali Community in the UK: What We Know and How We Know it* (London: Information Centre About Asylum and Refugees in the UK [ICAR], June 2004).

THE ROMA: Jan and Vera's Story

Jan and Vera, in their mid twenties, fled their village in eastern Slovakia in 1997 with their two young daughters after racist attacks. At the time of this interview, they were living in Dover awaiting a decision on their asylum application.

> Vera: I was attacked when I was walking home from the market on my own. Some skinheads beat me with a baseball bat and knocked out my four front teeth. A month later Jan was set upon on his way back from work and had his arm broken. Both times we went to the police and they shrugged their shoulders and said 'What do you expect us to do about it?' We were not surprised. Our home had already been petrol

bombed five times and five times the police were called and shrugged their shoulders.

Jan: It got so bad, we couldn't go out into the streets or on the bus. More and more shops had signs in the windows saying 'No Gypsies'. Our oldest child was taunted and spat at by the white children at her school. Our Slovak neighbours were sad to see us go but they were afraid of being attacked too because they were friends with Romanies. When we first arrived here, I thought England was paradise. Everyone was smiling at my children. And it makes me feel happy to see other black people here, people who look like us.

Josef, from a nearby town, tells a similar story.

Josef: What finally made us decide to move was when my wife Erika was thrown out of a moving bus by skinheads. She was badly hurt. A few weeks later, there was a knock on the door by men saying they were the police. When I opened the door, masked skinheads barged in, kicking and beating me and Erika. One of them grabbed our eight-year-old daughter Tina and held a gun to her head. They shouted and threatened us and then they left. We were so shaken by this that we left our home and moved from one town to another, hiding in the cellars of friends' houses. We didn't want to leave our home, our friends and our lives behind. People like the National Front think we came here because we want money but we had money in Slovakia. No, it's not that. We're here because we were afraid of being killed.[12]

In a number of ways, there are strong parallels between the Roma and the Jews of Europe. They are both culturally diverse people who have experienced centuries of persecution, social segregation and forced exiles. They have both faced centuries of extreme hatred and abuse institutionally as well as individually . And both groups were victims of the most highly organised and wide-scale genocide in human history. In the absence of reliable figures, estimates of Roma murdered by the Nazis during the Holocaust range from half a million to 1.5 million.

But to draw parallels beyond those would be to distort their extremely divergent realities past and present. Perhaps the most fundamental distinction is this: while the Jews have settled in established communities around the world and were granted a national homeland by the United Nations in 1948, there is no Jerusalem for the Roma people. The diaspora is their home, a forbidding place where you are forced to live in ghettoes; where you are considered second-class citizens and designated educationally subnormal. It is a place where you are assaulted by police and fellow citizens with impunity and without provocation, and where you are moved on from one town to another with unrelenting regularity because no community wants you near them.

Background

It is likely that the diverse groups of people generically known as Roma have their roots in India, where they lived as low caste Hindus. A mass exodus at around AD1000 scattered them westward, probably as a result of their being recruited – or dragooned – into a mercenary Indian army repelling Muslim invaders. They moved on to Persia, Armenia, Byzantium and finally, in the fourteenth century, to Europe. There, they were banned and expelled from one place to another which, say historians, was the origin of their nomadic lifestyle rather than an intrinsic desire to be on the move. Ethnically and culturally diverse because of this constant migration, they nonetheless possess an ethnic identity and a number of different dialects based on ancient Hindi and Punjabi, mixed with vocabulary adopted as a result of their regional migrations.

Banned continually from towns and villages throughout Europe, and even enslaved in Romania, they have traditionally lived on the margins, making a living as itinerant scrap merchants, metalworkers, circus hands, horse dealers, pedlars and beggars. Figures are notoriously unreliable as public records, government databases and social statistics tend to omit Roma completely or else classify them as 'other'.[13] However, from the information available it is possible to give approximations of current population figures. In total, there are between seven and eight and a half million Roma in Europe:[14] the majority live in central and eastern Europe: 2,500,000 in Romania, 800,000 in Bulgaria, 600,000 in Hungary and between 480,000 and 520,000 in Slovakia. There are slightly lower numbers in the Czech Republic and Poland.[15]

Persecution

The Roma suffer wide-scale economic and social deprivation and discrimination in employment, housing and education. Unemployment is ubiquitous, poverty its inevitable consequence and the breeding ground for criminality, mainly petty theft. Forced evictions from their homes, expulsions from town, sometimes with the approval of local mayors, physical assault and murder by skinheads, neighbours and even the police – all are occurrences that the Roma of Europe are subjected to, to varying degrees. In some areas they are excluded from public places. When they are caught for stealing and other small offences, they receive unusually harsh prison sentences and higher fines than the indigenous population.[16] Consequently, there are more Roma in central and eastern European prisons than any other minority group. Human rights group Helsinki Watch reports that 60 per cent of men in Hungarian prisons are Roma, while Romani women account for a quarter of women prisoners in Spain, even though Roma make up only 1.5 per cent of the population.[17]

Institutionalised racism in the education system means that in some countries Roma children are segregated from their white peers. In Ostrava in the Czech Republic, for instance, Roma children are 23 times more likely to be sent to special schools for the 'mentally retarded' than their white peers. In Hungary a petit apartheid system operates in some schools where a 'whites only' policy means that Roma children are barred from the canteens and gyms.[18]

Physical attacks come from all quarters. HOST, a Czech non-governmental organisation, recorded 1,250 racially motivated attacks against Roma between 1991 and 1997.[19] The police are also implicated in physical mistreatment that is, in some places, routine. To complain to the police about them is to invite further violence. The following are just a few incidents documented by Amnesty International:

- In *Hungary* a Romani funeral wake in 2001 was raided by around 80 police officers, who set about assaulting the mourners and others in the immediate vicinity. One of the funeral guests, so badly beaten that he required hospitalisation, had accused four police officers of torturing him two years earlier. The policemen's trial for that incident had been scheduled for two months after the funeral raid and one of the accused took part in the assault. The four officers who stood trial were given suspended sentences or fines although they were convicted of intimidation and assault.

- In *Slovakia* in the same year, a Rom (singular for Roma) died after being beaten while tied to a radiator in a police cell. He and his two sons had been arrested the previous day after making a complaint against a local police officer. A senior investigator reported that the man had *asked* to be tied to the radiator.

- In *Greece* some Roma have been designated living areas in what a Council of Europe expert has called 'institutionalised apartheid'. Others are routinely harassed by police during raids and, in 2001, an unarmed Rom was shot and killed by police when he failed to stop for a police patrol. The police officer was charged with murder but released on bail five days later and returned to service.[20]

Public opinion shows that anti-Roma sentiment runs strong through eastern and central European societies. Recent polls show that 91 per cent of Czechs have a 'negative view' of the Roma; polls from Hungary show similar findings.[21]

Arrival in Britain

The UK government has been intent on reducing the numbers of Roma asylum seekers coming here, particularly those from the Czech Republic. In July 2001 the Home Office received permission from the Czech authorities to place British immigration officers at Prague Airport in order to screen all passengers flying to the UK. Those who said their intent was to claim asylum were prevented from doing so by officials stamping their passport with a 'refusal of leave to enter', which would signal to the airline that they should be barred from boarding the flight.

The European Roma Rights Centre monitored the operation in the first three months of 2002 and found that 68 out of 78 Roma were prevented from getting on their flights to Britain, in contrast with 14 out of 6,170 non-Roma. As Law Lord Baroness Hale of Richmond put it, this made 'any individual Roma 400 times more likely to be rejected than any individual non-Roma'. She was one of the law lords who ruled in 2004 that the Home Office intervention at Prague Airport was, in her words, 'inherently and systematically discriminatory and unlawful'. Shami Chakrabarti, director of Liberty, said the ruling illuminated 'the racism at the heart of the government's asylum policy. The message was absolutely clear: "Roma not welcome in the UK." '[22]

The greatest numbers of Roma asylum seekers flowing into the UK came in 1998, leading to the temporary restrictive operation quoted above as well as to visa restrictions imposed on people coming from Slovakia. Because the British government considered the majority of asylum applicants from Poland, the Czech Republic, Romania, Hungary and Bulgaria to be bogus, motivated by economic or social concerns rather than the experience or the fear of persecution, there have been virtually no applications granted to Roma asylum seekers from these countries since 2000. This is due to those countries being on a 'white list' of countries believed to be safe and governed by the rule of law, compiled by the Home Office. Lord Avebury, who sat on the All-Party Parliamentary Group for Roma Affairs in Stage One Accession Countries, has called on EU member states to attack the root causes of the asylum claims rather than spending so much time and energy trying to keep Roma out of their countries. 'People should connect the influx of Romani asylum seekers with the failure of states concerned to eliminate inequality. If countries eliminated violence and discrimination, people wouldn't be asking for asylum.'[23] Since 2003 other countries with Roma populations, including Albania, Bulgaria, Serbia and Romania, have been added to the white list.[24] But with the accession of the Czech Republic, Slovakia and Poland, among other states, into the EU in 2004, Roma are now able to legally live in the UK without having to face asylum claim rejections.

Given the continuing institutionalised social and economic exclusion of Roma throughout Central and Eastern Europe due to ingrained racial prejudice, the interpretation of what constitutes persecution begs clarification.

OTHER MAJOR REFUGEE GROUPS SINCE THE SECOND WORLD WAR

The reception of refugees from eastern Europe after the war was a far cry from how asylum seekers are received today, largely due to the Cold War politics of the time. The horrors of Nazism followed by the repression and brutality of the Soviet regimes helped to excite enormous sympathy for those fleeing countries behind the 'iron curtain'. The International Refugee Organisation (the forerunner of the United Nations High Commission for Refugees, UNHCR), established resettlement programmes which involved a number of countries agreeing to take set numbers of refugees. Between 1947 and 1951 more than a million European refugees were resettled, the over-whelming majority of them outside Europe. Those who settled in the 1940s and 50s are now experiencing life as older refugees,* with its associated isolation and low income and the additional 'double jeopardy' of ageism and racism experienced by most black and minority ethnic elders. **

Poles

Between 1940 and 1950 210,000 Polish refugees and their dependants arrived in the UK. They came for different reasons: some were fleeing Nazism before the outset of the war, others were Displaced Persons (DPs) from camps in the British zone of Germany in the immediate aftermath of the war, and still others came as political refugees from the Soviet occupation of Poland. Some who had been in the Polish armed forces had suffered enormous hardships as deportees to Siberia after Russia had invaded Poland until an amnesty allowed them to return to fight the Nazis. Together, these Poles constituted the largest refugee group to arrive here after the war.

As well as large numbers who had been in the armed forces, many others had been government officials up to the time of the Nazi invasion of their country. Because of their show of strong solidarity with British forces during the war, the Poles who made it to this country were given preferential treatment compared to many other refugee groups. The 1947 Polish Resettlement Act entitled them to employment and to welfare benefits, which helped them to integrate successfully into British society. Even so, finding employment was not easy and most wound up in unskilled or manual jobs doing work that the English didn't want to do.[25]

*As 'age' is both a social construct and a chronological definition it is problematic to assume the concept of 'old people' as it applies in our society. Life expectancy varies hugely between countries. The standard definition of 'older' as being those over retirement age is not always suitable for members of refugee communities who may have aged earlier owing to economic hardships, traumatic experiences during escape and the dislocation of subsequent exile. (Older Refugees in Europe Survey Results & Key Approaches, ECRE Asylkoordination Osterreich, December 2002 .)

** Adapted from *Triple Jeopardy: Growing Old in a Second Homeland*, London: Centre for Policy on Ageing, 1985.

Hungarians

Between 170,000 and 200,000 Hungarians fled their country after the 1956 popular uprising against the Soviets, who had 'liberated' the country from the Nazis and then installed their own brand of totalitarianism. Thousands were killed when Soviet tanks were called in to quash the rebellion which followed the removal (and subsequent execution) of the reformist leader Imre Nagy six months earlier, and hundreds of thousands of dissenters fled the country into neighbouring Austria. It was from there that most came into this country.

The west was overwhelmed with sympathy for the Hungarians fleeing Communist repression. Even so, the UK government only agreed initially to accepting 2,500 refugees. That number was quickly exceeded and by 1959 had risen to over 21,000. After some re-emigration to North America, South Africa and the Antipodes as well as voluntary returns to Hungary and other eastern European countries, the number that eventually settled here was 14,500.[26] The official agency responsible for the resettlement of the Hungarians from refugee camps in Austria to Britain was the British Council for Aid to Refugees, the precursor to the Refugee Council. Numerous voluntary organisations were involved in relief and resettlement work as well.

Unlike the Poles, the Hungarians were mainly industrial workers for whom, in the late 1950s, there was no shortage of blue collar jobs.[27] They slotted into them with relative ease.

Chileans

In the same year that the expelled Ugandan Asians arrived in London, a bloody coup led by General Augusto Pinochet heralded the start of a brutal military dictatorship in Chile that was to last seventeen years. A reign of terror and repression descended on the country, beginning with the assassination of the democratically elected Marxist president Salvador Allende. Thousands fled as many others would flee over the next decade from similarly fascist regimes that overthrew governments in Argentina, Uruguay and elsewhere in Latin America.

Exact figures are unknown but tens of thousands of Chileans, most of them intellectuals and political opponents to the junta, fled to Spain, France and Sweden. In Britain the Conservative government of Edward Heath was grappling with the influx of Ugandan Asians and the unpopular response to them and was distinctly disinclined to open the doors further, let alone to opponents of a regime that it had formally recognised. When Labour came to power the following year, Harold Wilson's government cut the UK's ties with Chile and declared its sympathetic view of asylum applications from the country. Even so, it restricted the grounds and conditions for successful applications. Official figures put the number that came between 1973 and 1979 at 3,000. By the end of the 1980s some 750 had gone back.[28]

The role of voluntary organisations and Chilean Solidarity Committees in Britain was pivotal in bringing endangered dissidents to Britain and helping them resettle. The World University Service arranged international student scholarships that would satisfy the Home Office's selection process, helping students and academics to come here as political refugees and then offering them various training programmes that would make them employable. Formal responsibility for the reception and resettlement of Chileans came from the conglomerate of small voluntary organisations called the Joint Working Group for Refugees from Chile.[29]

Afghans

The decade-long Soviet occupation that began in 1979 left the country in anarchy and discord. Afghanistan become a land laid waste by the Russians and Americans playing out their cold warfare. Once the American-backed mujahideen, aided by Osama bin Laden, chased the Soviet troops out in 1989, the circumstances were ripe for a bloody civil war between opposing factions backed by Pakistan and Iran. The latter group prevailed, helping to sweep the radical Islamic Taliban

movement to power in 1996.[30] Through the 1990s huge numbers of people fled the fighting and repression. Iran and
Pakistan each hosted three million Afghan refugees; by 2001
Afghans had also become the largest national group seeking
asylum in the industrialised world, totalling 238,000.[31]

Following claims that Osama bin Laden had coordinated
the September 11 attacks from Afghanistan, the US invaded the
country a month later. Again, parts of the country were
destroyed in military action ostensibly being taken to flush
out bin Laden and his followers. In a few weeks, the Taliban
regime was toppled. But the dangerous situation did not end
there, nor has it today. Difficult social, economic and security
conditions remain, particularly in the south and southeast of
the country.

However, the relatively improved situation has meant that
asylum applications to western countries have dropped by
more than 80 per cent in the last three years and the number
of voluntary repatriations under the auspices of UNHCR has
been unprecedented: 4.2 million Afghans have returned home
since 2002 and at least half a million more were expected by
the end of 2005.[32]

These trends have been mirrored in the UK where, since
1994, a total of 34,000 Afghan asylum seekers have been
received. Since the end of 2002 the numbers applying for
asylum have been declining dramatically. While the numbers
peaked in 2001 with 9,000 cases, in 2004 they had dropped to
1,400. Although accurate figures are not available, the Refugee
Council quotes estimates of the numbers of Afghans living
here today to range between 40,000 and 70,000. There have
been concerns from various organisations, including Amnesty
International, about the forced return of asylum seekers from
Afghanistan whose claims have been rejected by the Home
Office. The Afghan Association of London agrees, citing 'the
ongoing military operations across different parts of the country, the lack of infrastructure, the existence of millions of
buried landmines causing casualties on a daily basis, the consequences of serious drought in recent years, severe political

instability and human rights abuses perpetrated, in some cases deliberately, by individuals'.[33]

The UK's shift in asylum policy, the development of a common asylum system among European Union member states and their echoes of each other will be discussed in the next chapter.

NOTES

1 S. Sanchez, 'Walking away from war: One woman's flight from the regime of Ugandan dictator Idi Amin'. Available at http://gseweb.harvard.edu/~t656_web/peace/Articles_Spring_2003/Sanchez_Sonya_WomanFleesUganda/htm (accessed 11 October 2007).

2 L. K. Narayan, *Indian Diaspora: A Demographic Perspective*, Occasional Paper 3, Centre for the Study of Indian Diasporas, University of Hyderabad, India (late 1990s).

3 Available at http://news.bbc.co.uk/onthisday/hi/dates/stories/august/7/news id_2492000/2492333.stm and http://www.le.ac.uk/pluralism/Religious%20 buildings.pdf (accessed on pp. 13–16).

4 Available at http://news.bbc.co.uk/1/hi/uk/2619049.stm (accessed 11 October 2007).

5 Hermione Harris, *The Somali Community in the UK: What We Know and How We Know It* (Information Centre about Asylum and Refugees in the UK [ICAR] 2004).

6 V. Robinson, 'Identifying modes of good practice in refugee dispersal and concentration'. Available at http://ralph.swan.ac.uk/refugeedisp/home.htm (accessed 11 October 2007).

7 Ibid.

8 Available at www.eurozine.com/article/2007-04-06-tripathi-en.html and www.bbc.co.uk/leicester/around_leicester/2007/09/ugandan_asians_leicester _changes.shtml/.

9 G. Bhattacharyya, L. Ison, and M. Blair, *Minority Ethnic Attainment and Participation in Education and Training: The Evidence* (London, DfES Research Topic Paper RTP01-03, 2003).

10 Harris, *The Somali Community*, pp. 49–50.

11 Available at www.crisisgroup.org/library/document/africa/horn_of_africa/ 095_counter_terrorism_in_somalia.pdf pp.1–2.

12 R. Klein, 'Paradise is where people smile at our children', *Times Educational Supplement*, 9 January 1998.

13 C. Clark, 'Counting backwards: the Roma 'numbers game' in central and

eastern Europe', *Radical Statistics Journal* 69 (Autumn 98). Available at www.radstats.org.uk/no.069/article4/.htm (accessed 11 October 2007).

14   J. R. Liegeois, *Roma, Gypsies and Travellers* (Council of Europe 1994).

15   R Klein, 'On the Move' *Times Educational Supplement*, 19 March 2004.

16   M. Brearley, *The Roma/Gypsies of Europe: A Persecuted People*. Institute of Jewish Policy Research, Report No. 3, December 1996.

17   Klein, 'On the Move', *Times Educational Supplement*, 19 March 2004.

18   Klein, op. cit.

19   ERRC (European Roma Rights Centre), Autumn 1997.

20   Available at http://web.amnesty.org/wire/February2002/Europe_Roma (accessed 11 October 2007).

21   G. Younge, 'Shame of a continent', *Guardian*, 8 January 2003.

22   A. Travis, 'An Asylum Operation Racist, say Law Lords', *Guardian*, 10 December 2004.

23   Institute of Race Relations, www.irr.org.uk/2003/april/ak000004.html.

24   ICMPD (International Centre for Migration Policy Development) *Current Roma Migration from EU Candidate States* (Vienna 2001) and *Britain fast tracks Roma back to discrimination,* 1 April 2003 Saleh Mamon, www.jcwi.org. uk/archives/ukpolicy/ho_17june03.pdf.

25   Tony Kushner and Katherine Knox, *Refugees in an Age of Genocide* (London, Frank Cass, 1999), pp. 225-6.

26   Ibid, p. 248.

27   'Hungarian Refugees in Britain', Refugee Council, ref RH/QU 59.2, p. 2.

28   Home Office Quota Resettlement Scheme, www.unhcr.org.uk/resettlement/ home_office_scheme.html/history.

29   Ibid.

30   Javed Nazir, 'A Pakistani Perspective. Afghanistan: Past, Present and Future', *Journal of the International Institute*, Vol. 9, no. 2, available at http:// www.umich.edu/~iinet/journal/vol9no2/nazir.html.

31   www.hrw.org/backgrounder/refugees/afghan-bck1017.htm#_ (accessed 12 October 2007).

32   Ibid.

33   Afghan Association of London Position Statement on the Return of Afghan Refugees, 30 April 2003, available at www.jeanlambertmep.org.uk/down loads/other/0304afghan_aziz.htm

CHAPTER FOUR

Claiming Asylum in the UK

1951 UNITED NATIONS CONVENTION ON REFUGEES

THIS international instrument has been both the foundation of refugee law worldwide and a cornerstone of human rights legislation[1] for over half a century, safeguarding the rights of those who have a well-founded fear of being persecuted for reasons of race, religion, nationality, membership of a particular social group or political opinion. It calls upon states who commit to it to protect refugees and treat them as equal members of society. The United Nations drafted and adopted the Convention in the wake of the mass displacement of between seven and nine million people after the Second World War, around two million of whom became refugees. The Protocol relating to the Status of Refugees, added in 1967, widened the scope of the Convention to include any people, anywhere in the world, who match the original criteria and in 1969 the Organisation of African Unity added another Convention that covered the specific issues of refugees in Africa. As of 1999 134 states had acceded to the Convention and Protocol.

While humanitarianism was a strong underpinning of the 1951 Convention, there was another – ideological – agenda. The Cold War was an era in which the West was keen to provide refuge to people fleeing the Communist regimes within the Soviet empire. But since the collapse of the Soviet Union globalisation has superseded the old polarisation, with mass migration and numerous regional conflicts replacing superpower stand-offs. Some critics of the Convention say that, with this changing world, the document has become outdated and irrelevant.

UK LAW

Since 1996 a succession of laws has been introduced to deter asylum seekers from coming to Britain and, if they do arrive here, to support them at a level that British citizens would not find acceptable for themselves. These laws are only the progression of a trend that had been in the ether for decades: the retreat from the post-war spirit of humanity that underpinned the 1951 UN Refugee Convention and the incremental hardening of attitude and of heart towards these most vulnerable of people. Humanity has given way to distrust and dislike.

The Asylum and Immigration Act 2004 is the third major law on asylum passed in the last five years and the fifth in eleven years. It was whisked through Parliament in near record speed. The initial consultation period of less than twelve weeks left little time for analysis and consideration. Although shorter than previous bills, it has gone further than any of its predecessors in restricting both the right to asylum and the rights of asylum seekers.

The following are key points of the Act and responses to them (italicised) from the Refugee Council, the UK's leading refugee rights body.[2]

The Act:

- criminalises asylum seekers arriving without official documents, i.e. passports and proof of identity in the absence of 'reasonable excuse'. Individuals may be arrested without a warrant if an immigration officer suspects that they have broken the law. The penalty is a fine and/or imprisonment of up to two years. Children aged ten and over, including those travelling unaccompanied, are subject to this law and can be convicted. While it may be considered in their defence if they can show that they travelled on false documents for all purposes during their journey or, conversely, that they travelled without an immigration document, it is an offence for them to have deliberately destroyed their original documents unless they can prove 'reasonable cause'. Being told to do so by the smuggling agent does not constitute 'reasonable cause'.

This measure could, in effect, penalise refugees for behaving like refugees . . . [People travel without documents] because of the impossibility of obtaining a passport from the very authorities that are responsible for the acts of persecution from which people are fleeing. There should be an absolute defence in all cases of unaccompanied children. The insistence on producing documents particularly penalises women, who are less likely to have access to their own documents. Often, they need the permission of a male relative to apply for a passport.

- puts an onus on asylum seekers to conform to behaviour that immigration officials consider credible, including a requirement to answer all questions posed by immigration officials.

The traumatising effects of torture and the residual fear that asylum seekers carry with them often makes it difficult for them to disclose and discuss their experiences. This is particularly the case with women who have been raped or otherwise abused and who feel, along with other responses, intense shame.

- criminalises people who traffic others in, within or out of the UK in order to exploit them.

While useful, the Act doesn't adequately protect the women and girls who are the key victims of traffickers. They require special measures, such as support and accommodation.

- insists that people claim asylum in the first safe country they reach.

International law does not stipulate this and it is not reasonable to expect people to do this. An asylum claim is no less credible if people wait till they arrive in the UK before making it.

- withdraws state support (accommodation and subsistence) from failed asylum seekers with families fourteen days after they have received their decision. If necessary, children will be taken into care to safeguard their welfare. Under Section 55 of the previous asylum legislation (the Nationality, Immigration and Asylum Act 2002), those who had not applied for asylum within three days of arrival were denied access to government support.

Removal of support from destitute asylum seeker families in the UK is, in the words of the Refugee Council, inhumane. A Refugee Council report that surveyed 130 organisations working with asylum seekers showed than 74 per cent were dealing with people who were forced to sleep rough and go hungry. A Court of Appeal ruling in the case of Secretary of State for the Home Department vs Limbeuela on May 21 2004 concluded that withholding support could be in breach of Article 3 of the UK Human Rights Act 1998. It determined that the Government should grant support to applicants unless it is certain that they have an alternative source of income available to them. This judgment has led to the Home Office agreeing to take a less restrictive approach when deciding whether a person has applied for asylum as soon as 'reasonably practicable'.

- states that 'hard case' support for failed asylum seekers who cannot be deported because of unstable circumstances in their home country is conditional on participation in voluntary community service (defined as 'activities that appear to the Secretary of State to be beneficial to the public or a section of the public').

Threatening to remove food and shelter if voluntary service is not carried out could flout articles 3 and 4 of the European Convention of Human Rights by being interpreted as forced labour and inhuman or degrading treatment. (In reality, enforced community service has never been implemented due to a lack of support from the voluntary sector.)

- repeals a previous feature of the 1999 Act that allowed people awarded refugee status to receive backdated payment of full income support from the date of the asylum claim.

Refugees should not be penalised in terms of benefit payment as a result of delays in processing their application.

- gives unprecedented powers of arrest, entry, search and seizure to immigration officers for immigration-related offences.

These are extremely wide powers that entitle immigration officers to arrest people without warrant if they are suspected of any of the listed criminal offences as well as to enter and search premises and seize any incriminating evidence. It is questionable whether the implementation of these sweeping powers will be subject to scrutiny.

- allows immigration authorities to remove asylum seekers to a safe third country designated by the Secretary of State as conforming to the Refugee Convention and the European Convention on Human Rights, within the EU as well as outside it. This can be done without in-depth consideration of their asylum claim or right of appeal against being sent to a particular country.

Removal to a safe third country without the right to appeal could infringe fundamental human rights. No country can be assumed to be safe for all people all of the time and with no requirement that the country is a signatory to the Refugee Convention, there is no proof that their rights would be respected and upheld. The criteria for designating countries safe is unclear and could have more to do with political or trade interests than with human rights. The Refugee Women's Resource Project, Safe for Whom? Women's Human Rights in 'Safe List' countries: Albania,

Jamaica and Ukraine, 2004 *illustrates the degree to which human rights are absent in so-called safe countries to which women have been returned.*

- introduces the use of electronic monitoring/tagging of asylum seekers over the age of 18 who have been subject to residence restrictions and need to report regularly to the authorities. The government believes it will help in managing these people who need to be available at specified times for interview, for appeal and possibly for their removal.

Because tagging has until now only been used in this country in criminal cases, the use of electronic monitoring to supervise the movements of asylum seekers could further stigmatise them socially.

Plans for a radical change of direction in UK asylum procedure, entitled *A New Vision for Refugees*, were leaked to the press at the beginning of 2003.[3] The Cabinet Office and Home Office policy paper was based on introducing two new strategies, regional protection zones (RPZs) and transit processing centres (TPCs). RPZs were intended to be situated in regions of armed conflict or natural disaster. Refugees or internally displaced people, it was envisaged, would be protected and housed there until they could be resettled in their country of origin. TPCs would be located near external borders of the European Union and would essentially function as detention centres in which asylum seekers arriving in the UK or elsewhere in the EU would be sent to await the processing of their asylum application. If their asylum claim was accepted, they would be resettled somewhere in the EU on a 'burden-sharing' basis. If their claim was rejected, they would either be deported to their home country or be protected temporarily until such a time as they could be repatriated.

These plans, from which UNHCR has distanced itself without condemning them categorically, have been dropped in their original form although the UK government is in the process of developing a regional protection programme which some EU countries may use as models themselves (see European Union Policy).

EUROPEAN UNION LAW

Just as the UK and all EU member states have their own national laws regarding asylum, so does the EU as a united body. And just as the UK has introduced laws that have progressively moved back from the spirit of the UN Convention on Refugees, edging away the much-vaunted welcome mat inch by inch to the extent that it is no longer visible, so has the European Union been working assiduously to erect a fortress around its borders to keep out the persecuted and desperate from around the world.

The parallel approaches to asylum legislation are no coincidence. Both have been driven by fallacies and misinformation from the major political parties as well as from the popular press. Both Britain and Europe believe themselves to be sagging under the weight of 'bogus' asylum seekers, depicted as ruthless opportunists who are unable to fit into European society. The events surrounding 9/11 have given this view added impetus as 'the other' has taken on a new sense of threat.

What every member state of the EU, including the UK, seems to be in the grip of is a delicate balancing act between controlling illegal immigration and fulfilling its duty to provide access to protection for genuine refugees. Increasingly, the two are merging to the detriment of those seeking asylum, with strict immigration controls in place that in practice deny sanctuary to those who need and are entitled to it under international law.[4]

The true numbers of asylum seekers in Europe come as something of a surprise, given the hysterical rhetoric in which they are couched. The former UN High Commissioner for Refugees, Ruud Lubbers, remarked that in 2004 the number of asylum seekers arriving in Europe was the lowest in sixteen years. Overall numbers dropped by an average of 18 per cent across EU member states. Whereas in 1992 approximately 680,000 people claimed asylum in EU countries, in 2003 there were fewer than 350,000. That level is manageable, according to Lubbers, and the EU should not be given carte blanche to renege on its commitment to human rights and the protection of refugees. In the 2003 European league table of numbers of asylum seekers, Germany had the highest with over 900,000. In Britain, there were 160,000, in Sweden 142,000, in France just over 100,000. Italy, which had a small established community of refugees, had one of the lowest intakes in Western Europe, with only 10,000. New asylum applicants to Britain in 2004 were 40,200, as opposed to just over 60,000 in the previous year and a peak of 103,000 in 2002, due to large numbers coming from Afghanistan and Iraq.[5] The situation is eminently fluid, with a constantly shifting picture both in terms of the eruptions of troubles around the world and the ever-tightening immigration and asylum controls being enforced throughout Europe.

Looked at from a global perspective, the proportion of asylum seekers given protection in EU countries is a fraction of that taken in by developing countries near conflict or disaster zones. Tanzania alone cares for the same amount of refugees as the entire European Union. Pakistan has the most, with over two million, followed closely by Iran.

EUROPEAN UNION POLICY

While Britain has had immigration legislation in place since the early twentieth century, asylum and immigration have only come onto the EU policy table since 1999. At the European Council in Tampere, Finland, heads of state agreed to the establishment of a common European asylum policy and system. It was decided to take these measures in a bid to find common solutions to the challenges that member states faced throughout the 1990s, with large influxes of asylum seekers and illegal migrants as a result of the Balkan wars, the Rwandan genocide and other conflicts outside EU borders.

The EU's stated precept in its Charter of Fundamental Rights is that protection, accommodation and social care must be provided to asylum seekers throughout the asylum claim procedure. It is up to the individual member states' laws how they will be provided for: whether in dedicated centres or by way of financial support that will allow them to rent accommodation. Once they are granted refugee status, they are eligible for the same 'basic help' and should be given the same rights (to health and social care, housing, education and employment) as all legal residents of all ages.[6]

However, there are regulations that the EU has put in place that contravene the principles underpinning the Convention and Charter. By putting up obstacles to prevent people from entering the EU in the first place, it is leaving desperate people to their own fate. Since 1995, for instance, it has been necessary for nationals of more than 130 states, including all the major refugee-generating countries, to obtain a visa before entering the EU, despite UNHCR's injunction that in those countries stricken by war, civil conflict and/or human rights violations, such requirements should not be made because of the dangers implicit in approaching foreign embassies.

Another barrier is the 2001 EU directive that, from September 2006, imposed fines on airlines, train and coach companies and other carriers who transport passengers without valid travel documents. This means that these companies are not allowed to carry asylum seekers who have no passports or visas which, as previously noted, is considered by refugee experts to be the position of the majority of bona fide asylum seekers.

Given such heavy restrictions, desperate asylum seekers with no hope of obtaining a legal passport or visa resort to people traffickers or smugglers to get into EU member states. New EU laws clamping down on illegal immigration and the trafficking of human beings are designed to stop the massive, organised crime operations that often cost vulnerable people exorbitant sums of money and, sometimes, their lives. Some of those unable to pay may find themselves forced into prostitution or criminal activities once they arrive at their destination.[7] However, the wholesale criminalisation of such means of entry also serves to criminalise asylum seekers themselves and undermine the validity of their claims.

HARMONISATION

The Common European Asylum System (CEAS), in development by the EU Asylum Procedures Directive, will ensure that member states, including the new accession states, harmonise their asylum systems in the following ways:

1. They will agree and set minimum standards for the reception of asylum seekers while their claim is processed in the host country.

2. They will agree on which country is responsible for examining an asylum claim based on a set of criteria including whether the asylum seeker has family in an EU country.

3. They will agree on a common definition of who is a refugee and what situations demand international protection as well as what rights and benefits are attached to different categories of asylum seeker.

4. They will determine minimum standards of the procedures for making decisions on asylum claims.

While stressing that all member states and acceding countries should ensure a 'dignified standard of living' to asylum seekers,[8] there are controversial elements in the CEAS that, if enacted, could erode international standards.[9] One of these is the restriction of in-country asylum appeals and the right to remain in the country during an appeal. Another is sending asylum seekers to another country deemed to be safe (known as a third country). This is Amnesty International's appraisal of the EU Asylum System:

National governments appear to be competing with each other to see how far they can lower standards of refugee protection in Europe in response to populist pressures. As a result, the EU's Common Asylum System is being held hostage. The proposed legislation would break the EU's own commitments set out in the Charter of Fundamental Rights . . . as well as individual EU governments' responsibilities under international law.[10]

The UK government took amended proposals on its concepts of regional protection zones (RPZs) and transit processing centres (TPCs) to the European Commission for discussion in 2003. Several papers followed but the UK proposals were not adopted. However, the German government took up the UK's concept and asked the EU to consider the idea of setting up camps in North Africa where asylum seekers could go to have their applications processed, rather than entering Europe.[11]

In an unprecedented move that could pave the way for action elsewhere in the EU, the Netherlands launched Europe's first mass expulsion of asylum seekers in February, 2004, when the Dutch Parliament voted to deport 26,000 failed asylum seekers.[12] These included Afghanis, Somalis and Chechens, whose countries were gripped in civil wars and lack functioning governments. This move followed the assassinations of right-wing anti-immigration politician Pym Fortuyn and controversial anti-Muslim film maker Theo Van Gogh. Among those uprooted was a young student from Angola who had lived in Holland for the previous seven years. In an interview with BBC Radio 4, she said: 'I don't have a home in Angola anymore. I have nowhere to go. I think it would be best if I was dead.'[13]

NOTES

1 Scottish Refugee Council, *The 1951 UN Convention*, www.scottishrefugee council.org.uk/Information/UN50.htm.
2 Refugee Council Briefing, *Asylum and Immigration Act 2004: Main Changes*

and Issues of Concern (London, Refugee Council, September 2004); 'Asylum seeker numbers drop sharply', www.refugeecouncil.org.uk/news/2005/Mar05/main_story.htm (accessed 12 October 2007), www.refugeecouncil.org.uk/policy/briefings/2004/act_2004.htm.

3 Human Rights Watch, 'An Unjuist "Vision" for Europe's Refugees', www.hrw.org/backgrounder/refugees/uk/introduction.htm (accessed 12 October 2007); www.statewatch.org./news/2003/mar/25asylum.htm.

4 European Council on Refugees and Exiles, *Introduction to Asylum in Europe* (London) www.ecre.org/factfile/facts.shtml.

5 *Refugees in the UK*, Refugee Women's Resource Project (Asylum Aid, 2004), www.asylumaid.org.uk/index.htm.

6 European Union, *EU Asylum Policy Guide* (Delegation of the European Commission to the Republic of Croatia 2004).

7 John Morrison and Beth Crosland, *The Trafficking and Smuggling of Refugees: The End Game in European Asylum Police?* UNHCR Report, 2000, www.ecre.org/eu_development/controls/traffick.pdf.

8 European Union, EU Policy Guide.

9 Amnesty International, 'European Union: Asylum – Amnesty International backs UNHCR criticism of EU asylum proposals', www.amnesty.org.uk/news_details.asp?NewsID=15018.

10 Amnesty International, European Union.

11 Kim Ward, *Regional Protection Zones and Transit Processing Centres* (London Information Centre about Asylum and Refugees in the UK [ICAR], 2004).

12 Ambrose Evans-Pritchard, *Telegraph*, (18 February 2004).

13 BBC Radio 4, 'The World at One', (30 January 2005).

CHAPTER FIVE

The Asylum Experience

GETTING HERE: FORCED OUTSIDE THE LAW

IF there is one word to describe the essence of the asylum system today, it is deterrence. It has become virtually impossible to enter the UK in a legal manner in order to claim asylum.[1] The Home Office has achieved its stated aim of reducing the numbers of asylum seekers 'dramatically': in the first three months of 2004, they fell by one fifth and the number of cases waiting for an initial decision was the lowest for a decade.[2] The reductions are due to two factors: having rolled out an ever-increasing number of obstacles to make it more and more difficult for people to get to this country is the first one. The second is the decrease in the numbers of refugees worldwide.[3]

Whereas until recently asylum could be granted to applicants coming from countries identified by the Home Office as posing dangers to its citizens as a result of, for instance, war or civil conflict – Libya, Liberia and Somalia came into this grouping – this is no longer the case. Because every case is considered on its own merit, those from areas of conflict may be sent back if their claims are not strong or credible enough. As a result, countries still in the chaotic aftermath of war, with roaming armed militias and gangs threatening the population, are no longer considered unsafe places to which to return their nationals. However, a new scheme for small numbers of groups of people considered 'exceptionally vulnerable' – victims of rape and torture – has been instituted jointly by the United Nations and the Home Office. It works to resettle those from strife-torn countries like Liberia and Congo who had been living in squalor in neighbouring refugee camps in danger of further persecution. To date, 115 have arrived under this resettlement programme. It is clear that the original aim of bringing over five hundred in the first year of the scheme and a thousand in the second will not be carried through because of the reluctance of local authorities around the country to house and support them.[4]

When conflicts erupt and numbers of refugees increase, visas are almost invariably introduced, which means that people arriving from strife-torn countries cannot enter Britain without acquiring a visa from the British embassy in their home country which may be almost impossible. In essence, the worse the human rights situation in a country, the more difficult it is to seek asylum in Britain.[5]

The prosecution of would-be asylum seekers entering the UK without a passport or other valid documents is another way of deterring people from coming. While there is a proviso for those with 'reasonable excuse' or a 'defence' that immigration officers could accept, it is very much open to interpretation. Officials may look at a case sympathetically, depending on circumstances, but the law says that people who are commanded by their agents/people smugglers to destroy their papers do not have 'a reasonable excuse'. The penalty is an unlimited fine and imprisonment for a maximum of two years. This problem has become particularly acute since the rise of global terrorism; the government's duty to protect its citizens becomes, it says, further complicated than it already is in the absence of proof of people's identities. Equally troubling for the Government is the perception, enforced by sensationalist media coverage, that it does not have proper procedures in place, leaving the population vulnerable and the situation chaotic.

The demand for official documentation is completely unrealistic, according to the United Nations High Commission for Refugees. 'In most cases, a person fleeing from persecution will have arrived with the barest necessities and very frequently without personal documents.'[6] Very few asylum seekers will possess passports because the issuing of visas, passports and other official documentation, such as birth certificates, is in the hands of the same government or regime from which the person is fleeing. Ironically, those who *do* arrive with documents are often suspected by UK immigration officers of not being bona fide asylum seekers.[7]

By implementing this law, the government appears not only to be contravening but actually subverting the spirit of the UN Convention on Refugees (Article 31) by further penalising people for coming from countries that abuse its citizens' civil rights. How they are meant to obtain official documents from a regime that denies its citizens their human rights including their access to official documents and the freedom to travel, is unclear.

Sairan, 34, is one of the many thousands who left her country, Iraq, in 2000 without bona fide documents because she had no alternative. Her story echoes many others who have been forced to enter Britain illegally because of lack of documents.

> I was a teacher near Suleimania in the north, where there are a number of Islamic militants. They came to school with guns one day and told me that I had to teach the Koran since I taught Arabic. I refused and they imprisoned me for two weeks in a damp room with no food. They wore masks and treated me roughly. They tried to change my thinking and said I had to wear a scarf or they'd kill me. I said no again. I thought to myself: if they kill me, it's only once. I was set free when a lot of students and people from the town came and demanded my release.
>
> After that, my family helped me escape to Turkey because we were afraid they would come for me again. I bought an illegal passport for $700 in Kurdistan. Under Saddam, we didn't have passports. It was like being in prison. So I had no choice but to buy an illegal one.
>
> Once I got to Turkey, I went to a sheikh who helped me and others from my town who had had to leave after being

threatened by the militants. He helped us find a people smuggler and we gave $5,000 to him. We were three families, a woman and a man. He put us into a lorry full of boxes. There was no toilet, no air. It was in April and it was very hot during the day and cold at night. We spent three nights in the lorry till we got to Italy. Then we changed to another lorry that took us to Calais.

There we stayed for two months at Sangatte *[the refugee centre, now closed down]*. They were good to us and gave us food there. We tried ten, twenty times to get to the border in lorries but the French police forced us out each time and then would drive us back to Sangatte. But we were desperate to leave France because they wouldn't let us stay there and we didn't want to be sent back to Iraq.

Finally, we paid extra money and were put into a box underneath a lorry, in the undercarriage. The people smuggler told us it was only twenty minutes from Calais to England, but I was afraid to go into the box. Just a month before, we'd heard that 56 Chinese had died in similar conditions. But finally, a child, a woman and I got into the small box and had to lie very still.

We went through the Channel Tunnel for twenty minutes and then the lorry stopped. The woman in the box with me started shouting to the driver to open the box but it seemed like the driver was worried and hesitated. Finally, he and two men opened the box and told us to go away quickly.

We came out of the station and saw some policemen. We asked them for the Home Office, which is what the smuggler told us to do. They were very helpful and took us to the police station. It was very late at night but they paid for a taxi driver to take us to the Home Office *[the Immigration Department at Lunar House, Croydon]*. We didn't know where that was but we arrived there, in Croydon, at 1.30 in the morning. The lady driver said she wouldn't leave us there alone all night, so she took us to the police station nearby. They gave us a room with blankets until the morning. My first impression of the British police was that they were so good, so helpful. The next morning we went to the Home Office. We stayed there for hours while they investigated us and then they gave us £8 each and told us to go to Croydon Refugee Council. The first thing they asked us when we arrived there was 'have you eaten?' They were so kind. They found us a B & B in Finsbury Park where we stayed for six months.

Sairan lived in a succession of temporary accommodations in London, from hostels to self-contained studio flats, before being housed in a short-term council flat in the London Borough of Camden.

> I have been given leave to remain for ten years. After that, I don't know what will happen to me. But however bad it is, it's nothing like Iraq. Saddam killed my aunty in Hilabja with the chemical bombs in 1998. Here, anything can happen but at least I'm free.[8]

It is increasingly the case that the route to the UK is a high stakes operation. Every year, thousands risk their lives and pay extortionate sums of money to a variety of people traffickers in order to flee their own countries for sanctuary here and in other countries in the west. In the past fifteen years at least 90 people have been killed trying to reach Britain as stowaways on planes, trains, trucks and boats. This figure is likely to be a gross underestimate; only a fraction of cases are actually reported in the press.[9]

Those killed were not criminals, unlike the people claiming to help them and the many thousands of desperate people around the world. The enormously risky routes they take to get here are not their choice of travel. Rather they, and the countless others who survive such perilous journeys, are forced to turn to people smugglers or so-called immigration agents because the legal barriers to getting into a safe country make their chances of gaining asylum extremely remote.

Q, from Somalia, tells a harrowing but not uncommon story of unscrupulous people traffickers playing a lethal game with people's lives:

> I remember living a [normal] life. Me, my husband and eight children . . . But the war breaks. We fled. Far away to south Somalia. Two months on, everything's out of hand. We run

away from the civil war – me, my husband and eight children . . . And we go from Somalia by boat towards Kenya. But
suddenly the boat is sinking. The boat is overloaded . . . The
boat broke. Water breaking into us . . . I can't swim. The boat
sinks. Who will rescue us? . . . two hundred people are dying,
drowning. I'm losing my family to the sea. Five of my
daughters are lost. And my eldest son, he's just begun his life,
he's finished university. He's lost. That makes six of my children. Dead in the sea, in one day . . . Suddenly, an Italian
tourist boat is passing . . . people come to rescue us. They grab
my baby, who I'm holding. And another child of mine . . . All
the time my baby's calling 'mama, mama'. Suddenly, I am
hauled into the boat like a baby myself . . . I am crying. My
whole body. Crying . . . I cannot forget that day. Although I'm
here before you today, you can't have imagined the life of one
Somalia woman . . . I am breaking the silence. The world
should know my life, my baby calling 'mama, mama'. The
world should hear this life. [10]

Thousands of people have taken similarly perilous escape
routes out of their countries to flee persecution and war.
Some, like the 58 Chinese migrants found asphyxiated in the
back of a lorry in Dover, penetrate our consciousness by the
particularly gruesome nature of their deaths. Many more are
unheard of or are quickly forgotten, like the Iraqi Kurd who
died in an attempt to smuggle himself to Dover by clinging to
the bottom of a lorry. Or the two Cubans who froze to death
after tucking themselves into the undercarriage of a plane
bound for London: at 30,000 feet they would have suffered
temperatures of minus 40 degrees Centigrade. The total documented deaths of asylum seekers between 1993 and 2002 are
2,406. These include death by asphyxiation, drowning, landmines, electrocution and exhaustion. Also included in this
number are 135 suicides by people either in detention or in
fear of deportation, which have occurred in Britain and on the
Continent.[11]

ONCE THEY HAVE ARRIVED . . .

Asylum applications can be made in a number of ways. The most immediate and straightforward is by going directly to an immigration officer at the port of entry (a channel port or an airport). Otherwise, it is done after arrival at an office of the Home Office Immigration and Nationality Directorate in Croydon, Liverpool or Solihull. This is known as in-country application. In both cases the Home Office will ask for documents to support the asylum claims. There is an exhaustive interview process, when dates and details are requested and photographs and fingerprints are taken. All port applicants and some in-country applicants receive a letter giving them permission to stay in the UK temporarily while the Home Office processes their application. If an immigration officer decides that an application can be settled quickly due to its being 'manifestly unfounded', the asylum seeker may be placed either in a reception centre or removal centre until the final decision is made.[12] Some, despite having committed no crime, are held in mainstream prisons, though those numbers have decreased since the expansion of detention centres.

After the preliminary interview, applicants are required to complete and return an extensive and detailed Statement of Evidence Form (SEF) within ten days. Specialist legal advice is required for filling out the form (it asks, for instance, what aspects of the Refugee Convention the claim relates to) and the SEF and supporting documents may need translation. However, the strict time limit of ten days makes this a difficult task to achieve. Failure to comply with the deadline results in automatic refusal of the application and possible removal from the country. So does any failure to comply with conditions such as keeping interview appointments or passing the ten-day limit for lodging an appeal.[13]

Whereas previously an asylum seeker could wait two years or longer for a decision to be made, the Home Office now aims to have applications processed in two months, and much quicker for those kept in detention. If an application is refused, some asylum seekers are denied the right to appeal because their home countries are included in a list of states considered to be safe by the British government. They may, however, be allowed to appeal from outside or even within the UK in exceptional circumstances. For those who come from countries not on this list, the right to appeal to the courts is allowed. An independent adjudicator hears cases within two months of the original decision and a final decision is made within two weeks of the appeal (it is possible to appeal this decision on a point of law).[14]

CATEGORIES OF STATUS

Until 2003 those who claimed persecution but failed to be awarded full refugee status could be granted *Exceptional Leave to Remain* (ELR) for an initial four-year period, after which they could apply for *Permanent Leave to Remain*. ELR has been replaced by a classification known as *Humanitarian Protection* (HP), which allows the applicant to live in the UK for a maximum of three years before their case is reviewed. If the situation in their home country has not improved over that period and if returning could mean endangering their life or liberty, the person can apply for *Indefinite Leave to Remain* (ILR). Somewhere between HP and ILR is *Discretionary Leave to Remain*, a less frequently awarded category for those who qualify for neither refugee status nor HP but who are allowed to stay for other reasons, such as strong community ties in the UK. This is initially granted for up to three years, during which time recipients can receive welfare benefits and are eligible to work. After a review, they may have their status extended for another three years, after which they can apply for ILR.

DETENTION

Under the regulations of the 2002 Nationality, Immigration and Asylum Act, asylum seekers may be:

- housed for up to six months in accommodation centres, which provide on-site health provision and schools
- held in detention or removal centres if their applications for asylum have failed or if they are considered 'high risk'. Detention is usually a precursor to deportation ('removal')
- removed to a 'safe third country' designated by the Home Secretary as a state that complies with the Refugee Convention and the European Convention on Human Rights. This may be to an EU country although others outside the EU may be used.

All asylum seekers are liable to detention at any point during their wait for a decision to be made on their application (although this happens to a relatively small number). This practice flouts UN High Commission for Refugees guidelines which state that detention should only be used in exceptional circumstances and never in mainstream prisons.[15] In addition, UNHCR calls the detention of minors 'undesirable' and 'a measure of last resort for the shortest appropriate period of time'.[16] Two women's testimonies offer a glimmer into the confusion, incomprehension and terror that come with the territory of being detained:

> They told me they will take me to another place but I didn't realise it was a detention centre with gates and security officers. It's hard, you feel like a criminal, it's not nice . . . At the beginning it was a bit easier because I thought they would accept my asylum claim. I thought this is okay, I will pay the price [by being kept in detention] . . . But after, when I realised they had decided to refuse my claim, it was horrible . . .

> They came to put me in detention in September. They didn't even write to me beforehand. It was Saturday. A woman and a man came here, they asked for my papers. I don't know who they were. They showed me an identity card like the police have. They asked me if I had a lawyer and where my children were going to school. But they didn't tell me anything.
> The next Wednesday morning, I was preparing to take my

children to school. I had not even brushed my teeth yet, I was bathing my baby. I heard someone knocking on the door. Ten people entered my home. They started to search all the rooms, everywhere. I was tortured like a dog. One of the police guys twisted my arm so badly I still feel the pain today. When I need to carry my child I have to use the other arm. They told me 'we are going to deport you back to your country'. Why didn't they tell me before that they didn't want me to stay here?

My children started to cry and they said to them 'shut up'. All day long my children didn't get anything to eat. Just the thought of it gives me pain. My baby, they didn't even give me any nappies for my baby. He peed on my lap. They didn't even give me milk [for the baby].

Now I am taking medications all time. I have headaches. My children, whenever they hear someone knocking on the door, they run off in the other rooms. They are frightened whenever they see a policeman.

They kept us in the van till midnight . . . My children have asthma . . . and were crying because they felt suffocated in the van. But they locked the van and they left, they left us there. I was tired, my children were tired. At midnight, they took us to Dungavel *[Immigration Removal and Detention Centre in South Lanarkshire, Scotland].*[17]

Since 2000 ten asylum seekers and other foreign nationals have committed suicide in UK detention and removal centres. There are a number of probable causes: one is detainees' fears that they will be returned to the hands of their persecutors in their home countries. Another is that they are particularly vulnerable people, some of whom will have been tortured or otherwise abused, or have witnessed the abuse and murder of people close to them. Yet another is the reported mistreatment of detainees by custody officers at these centres.[18]

GETTING THE BASICS

The Asylum Resources Directorate (formerly known as the National Asylum Support Service (NASS)) is a department run by the Immigration and Nationality Directorate of the

Home Office. It provides a basic welfare package to destitute asylum seekers who can prove that they have no means of support or that they will have none within two weeks of arrival in the UK. In theory all impoverished asylum seekers are eligible for basic subsistence payments and accommodation while their applications are being processed by the Home Office. No accommodation is supplied if there are friends or relatives with whom the applicant can stay. The payments available to asylum seekers amount to 70 per cent of the income support available to British citizens. In 2007 these are the weekly payments:

A couple: £63.07

A lone parent aged 18 and over: £40.22

A single person aged 25 and over: £40.22

A single person aged 18–25: £31.85

A single person aged 16–18: £34.60

Children under 16: £45.48

Where the ARD provides half or full board with accommodation, the payments are reduced accordingly.[19]

Research at the University of Leeds found that this level of benefit was not only unsustainable but actually promoted poverty and social exclusion. For those denied asylum but not sent home, the situation is even worse, driving them to rely on support from other asylum seekers or charities.[20]

Stringent restrictions on eligibility for government support came into force under Section 55 of the Nationality, Immigration and Asylum Act 2002. This regulation states that in-country applicants could only apply to the ARD if they could prove that they had requested asylum 'as soon as reasonably practicable' after arrival, in other words, that they had not spent time in the UK before applying for asylum. The excessively severe interpretation of this regulation meant that in 2003 approximately 9,000 asylum seekers were denied even the most basic means of support from the state and had to rely on charity and handouts from refugee welfare organisations.

After the furore in response to the harshness of Section 55, a test case brought to the Court of Appeal in May 2004 concluded that the Home Office was in breach of Article 3 of the European Convention on Human Rights. The case, brought on behalf of three asylum seekers, one of whom was a Rwandan Hutu woman who had been regularly raped and beaten by Tutsis in a refugee camp, has led to an amendment of Section 55, though not its eradication. From June 2004 the Home Office has had a duty to provide basic welfare services to asylum seekers, unless it believes that an individual has alternative means of support, i.e. night shelter, food and basic amenities.[21]

But it remains the case that there are thousands of asylum seekers around the country living in destitution, with no means of support from the government and no access to healthcare. The National Audit Commission estimates that a minimum of 283,000 asylum seekers, the vast majority of whom will have had their applications for asylum refused, are living in destitution. Errors in the initial screening process by immigration officers, compounded by inflexibility in investigating cases and local authorities' difficulties in supporting failed asylum claimants, have led to this situation.[21]

ACCOMMODATION: DISPERSAL

For those who are destitute and homeless the ARD provides emergency temporary accommodation and full board during the time it takes for their application for support and housing (as distinct from their asylum application) to be processed. While in this emergency accommodation asylum seekers are not given any financial means of support.

Once their application for support is approved they are 'dispersed', or offered accommodation in designated areas around the country. These areas are outside London and the southeast, where a large proportion of emergency and intermediate accommodation for asylum seekers has been located, unless there are 'exceptional circumstances' for them to remain in the area. Dispersal is the Home Office's response to the plight of local authorities in London and around the south coast, such as Dover, for whom demands on housing and social services, health and education for asylum seekers had become intense. The government's solution has been to spread – disperse – asylum seekers around the country, to areas with surplus housing. Often this has meant low-cost, hard-to-let housing stock and housing estates on the periphery of towns and cities, where there are high levels of unemployment, poverty and social exclusion. Since the government instituted the dispersal scheme, over 100,000 asylum seekers have been scattered to areas such as Glasgow, Wrexham, Liverpool and Newcastle, where there have been a number of murders and vicious attacks. Fewer have wound up in places like Burnley, Oldham Sunderland and Bradford: town names that have entered the public consciousness thanks to British National Party activity, racist attacks and riots.[23]

While the Home Office had envisaged a programme in which people from similar backgrounds would be 'clustered' together by country of origin and culture, the volume of demand for temporary housing has made this impossible. Refugee rights organisations have criticised the dispersal system for not taking into account applicants' social and cultural needs; a European report has called for a return to the original plan of cluster areas rather than basing the programme on the availability of housing.[24]

Not only does scattering asylum seekers lead to social isolation and the distress that this can cause, but an increasing number of people dispersed to neighbourhoods that lack established minority ethnic communities are reporting racist incidents. According to research carried out by the charity Refugee Action, asylum seekers are the victims of racial attacks and abuse across the UK on a daily basis. One in five of its clients has experienced some form of harassment and one in three are too frightened to leave their homes after dark. In

Plymouth official police figures in 2003 revealed between 22 and 30 racist attacks per month, many against asylum seekers. Refugee groups in the area suggest that the real figure could be as much as six times more; most go unreported because people are afraid of going to the police.[25] Half a dozen asylum seekers have been killed in racially motivated murders since 2001 in places where refugees were recent arrivals on the scene: Plymouth, Sunderland, Glasgow. In particular there has been a dramatic increase in racist attacks against Afghans and other Muslims since 11 September 2001, as in other countries across Europe.[26]

Despite evidence showing the negative effects of the dispersal policy, the government has new proposals to restrict the areas where people can settle once they receive refugee status. Those who were dispersed outside London and the southeast will not be allowed to return there to be housed in council accommodation.

HEALTH AND MENTAL HEALTH SERVICES

Health care for asylum seekers in the UK is often ignored or inappropriate or delivered too late. Asylum seekers come in a vulnerable state, sometimes traumatised after having been tortured, raped or psychologically abused. The physical and emotional toll taken by leaving their homes and travelling, often on arduous journeys, can exacerbate their fragile physical and mental state. A research paper by the British Medical Association (BMA) and the Medical Foundation for the Care of the Victims of Torture argues that their health may deteriorate once they have entered the UK. The inability to access services is aggravated by poor housing, poverty and depression due to previous experiences, social isolation caused by dispersal and a lack of translation and interpreting assistance.[27] A further factor is having poor or inappropriate services near their temporary (and often transitory) accommodation, particularly when they have pre-existing conditions such as tuberculosis that require consistent and sustained treatment.

All these factors may be particularly difficult for older people with little or no English and who suffer from chronic health problems.

People who have been imprisoned and/or tortured may also require specialist mental health services that, for a variety of reasons, they are not able to access. There are extremely good, dedicated clinics in Leeds and Folkestone, along with the Medical Foundation for the Care of the Victims of Torture in London, which has an international reputation as a centre of excellence. However, these facilities are under-resourced, in great demand and far away from those who have been dispersed to geographically far-flung towns in provincial England, Wales and Scotland.

The following are some of the case studies submitted by doctors and mental health workers to the BMA and Medical Foundation's dossier *Asylum Seekers and Health*:

> I saw an elderly woman living in temporary accommodation. She had severe curvature of the spine. I think she probably had polio as a child. She is completely alone and unable to communicate. She has major medical problems. We spend a lot of time trying to help her. I worry what will happen to her if she is dispersed.

> A client was 'dispersed' to Bradford. This man is a survivor of imprisonment and torture. His torture included being forced to eat food which had sharp wire hidden in it. Despite appeals from the Medical Foundation, this man was 'dispersed'. He has profound psychological problems and needs regular counselling sessions. He is also deeply concerned about his physical state and needs proper medical assessment and follow-up. When he arrived in Bradford, he walked 40 minutes to the local hospital and desperately tried to make himself understood . . . There is no money for fares and it is impossible for him to seek help for his psychological and physical problems without walking great distances when he is unwell. Efforts are being made to persuade the National Asylum Support Service to re-house him in London, where there will still be problems of no payment of fares and there may be problems of poor

accommodation, but at least there will be psychological and medical help at the Medical Foundation which he desperately needs.

[There] was a man with mental health problems who was 'dispersed' to a northern city where he knew no one and had no community support. His mental illness deteriorated. He began to eat poison and was picked up by the police as he walked on the motorway on his way back to London.[28]

A recent report highlights uncertainty among health professionals themselves about whether asylum seekers are entitled to NHS services.[29] Under both asylum legislation and the Human Rights Act 1998 refugees, as well as anyone who has formally applied for asylum or who has been granted Humanitarian Protection, are entitled to be registered with a GP and to receive free health care. Like UK citizens on benefit they are entitled to free prescriptions if they are receiving ARD benefits.

LIVING LIFE ON HOLD

Even though life on asylum seekers' benefits is unsustainable, the Home Office prohibits them from working or pursuing vocational training while they await a decision on their asylum application. No matter how long their case takes to be resolved, they are obliged to eke out an existence in a state of limbo, an alien world in which nothing is familiar, everything is beyond their means and where they have no role. The government has pledged to fast track applications, aiming to process them by two months. Whether this is achieved in all cases is open to question.

Permission to work is granted when an asylum seeker receives a positive decision on their application. This applies to everyone of working age in the family. Once they have refugee status, they can claim income support. In the meantime both asylum seekers and refugees can get guidance on English language and vocational courses from the Refugee Council or local Learning and Skills Council, as well as information about getting their qualifications recognised in this country. Meanwhile there is little support available for or directed towards those over official working age. Numbers are very small: in the year 2000 three per cent of asylum seekers were aged 50 and over and in the absence of such things as supportive social activities or language classes they are likely to be very isolated.[30]

Under the Asylum and Immigration Act (2004) failed asylum seekers who cannot be deported back to their potentially dangerous home countries are obliged to carry out community work. This is in exchange for what is called 'hard cases' support, which amounts to a minimum subsistence level for those in special need. The largest group in this category are Iraqis, whom the government has agreed not to remove while hostilities continue. The only organisation that agreed to provide community work opportunities was the YMCA but they have since withdrawn the offer, leaving the government with no partner to implement this plan.

APPEALS

Approximately one in five asylum applicants who have been initially rejected go on to win their appeals. According to the Refugee Legal Centre, this indicates flaws in the initial decision-making stages of the asylum process. They could be due either to legal representatives having inadequate information or insufficient time to consider it or pressures on the system to process applications more quickly.[31]

All failed applicants should be informed of their rights to appeal and told how to do so. In most cases they are given ten working days after receiving their rejection letter to lodge an appeal. There are two grounds for appeal: that the basis of the claim has not been fully considered, and that the protection offered by the Human Rights Act 1998 has not been upheld. New regulations prevent applicants from making more than one appeal in different courts.[32]

REMOVALS

When the Immigration and Nationality Directorate (IND) refuses an asylum application some people will be given the right of appeal, depending on the individual case. Those who are denied the right of appeal and who have no other basis on which to stay are told to leave the UK. If they wish, they can be helped to do so under the Voluntary Assisted Return Programme, which means that the government arranges their transport costs back to their home country. If they do not leave of their own accord they may be detained and removed by the IND.

There is documented evidence of detainees being treated with excessive force and other abuse by security staff in the process of removing them for deportation. The Medical Foundation found evidence to support clients' claims of excessive or gratuitous force in twelve out of fourteen cases over a period of fifteen weeks in 2004. One third sustained varying degrees of nerve damage consistent with the use of tight restraints or handcuffs applied too tightly. The doctors at the Medical Foundation accepted that some force or restraint was likely to be necessary in dealing with disruptive detainees but nevertheless recommended that the Home Office install CCTV cameras in the vans used for transport asylum seekers from detention to the airport for 'removal'. They also suggested automatic medical examination of asylum seekers after a failed removal attempt and a review of restraint techniques.[33] The Home Office has committed to installing cameras in the vans but has not agreed to the other recommendations.

NOTES

1 Immigration Advisory Service, *The Asylum Process*, www.iasuk.org/c2b/PressOffice/display.asp?ID=2188Type=2.

2 Directgov, 'Falling asylum figures confirmed' 25 May 2004, www.direct.gov.uk/Newsroom/NewsArticle/fs/en?CONTENT_ID=4013567&c.

3 In its latest report, the UNHCR states the number of refugees worldwide is

the lowest it has been for 26 years, dropping from 9.5 million in 2004 to 8.4 million in 2005. However, the number of refugees of concern to them has actually increased by over one million, to 20.8 million, largely due to internally displaced people: people living as refugees within their own countries. ('The State of the World's Refugees 2006; Human displacement in the new millenium', UNHCR, www.unhcr.org/static/publ/sowr2006/toceng.htm.)

4 Alan Travis, 'Most vulnerable refugees arrive under new scheme', *Guardian*, 1 November 2004.

5 Asylum Aid, 'Refugees in the UK', Refugee Women's Resource Project, Asylum Aid, London, February 2003, http://www.asylumaid.org.uk/publications.php?category=2&search=Search&page=3&page=4.

6 UNHCR, www.unhcr.org./excom/excom/3ae68cce4.html.

7 Frances Webber, 'Concern at new asylum measures', Independent Race and Refugee News Network, www.irr.org.uk/2003/december/ak00000.html (1 December 2003).

8 From a personal interview conducted by Reva Klein in London, March 2005.

9 Harmit Athwal, *Death Trap: The Human Cost of the War on Asylum*, Institute of Race Relations, (London, October 2004).

10 Hermione Harris, *The Somali Community in the UK: What We Know and How We Know It* (London Information Centre about Asylum and Refugees in the UK: [ICAR] 2004).

11 UNITED, *List of Documented Deaths* (Amsterdam, 2002), www.picum.org/DOCUMENTATION/listofdeaths.pdf (accessed 12 October 2007).

12 Migrant Helpline, Refugee Arrivals Project, Refugee Action, Scottish Refugee Council, Welsh Refugee Council, Refugee Council, *Applying for Asylum* (2003).

13 Asylum Aid, 'Refugees in the UK'.

14 In 2004 88 per cent of asylum applications were refused. About a fifth of these decisions were overturned on appeal. See http://news.bbc.co.uk/1/hi/uk_politics/4285431.stm (accessed 13 October 2007).

15 Oxfam, 'Myth 8: Asylum seekers should be locked up', www.oxfamgb.org/ukpp/safe/myths8.htm (accessed 13 October 2007).

16 UNHCR, www.unhcr.org./excom/excom/3ae68cc34.html.

17 Sarah Cutler and Sophie Ceneda, *They Took Me Away: Women's Experiences of Immigration Detention in the UK* (Bail for Immigration Detainees and the Refugee Women's Resource Project at Asylum Aid 2004).

18 Institute of Race Relations 'Failing the vulnerable: the death of ten asylum seekers and other foreign nationals in UK detention', posted on Independent Race and Refugee News Network 26 July 2004, www.irr.org.uk/2004/july/ak000016.html (accessed 13 October 2007).

19 http://oxfamb.org/ukpp/resources/downloads/poverty_report_july02.pdf, www.broadwaylondon.org/broadwayvoice/policy/asylum_final.pdf and www.bbc.co.uk/dna/actionnetwork/A2151785 (accessed 13 October 2007).

20 P. Dwyer *et al, Meeting Basic Needs? Exploring the Survival Strategies of Displaced Migrants,* Economic and Social Research Council (London, 2005).

21 www.building.co.uk/story.asp?sectioncode=306&storyCode=3037344 and www.ind.homeoffice.gov.uk/6353/12358/pb82.pdf.

22 Coventry Refugee Centre, *Destitution and Asylum Seekers: A Human Rights Issue* (Coventry, 2005).

23 Charlotte Granville-Chapman *et al, Harm on Removal: Excessive Force against Failed Asylum Seekers* (London, Medical Foundation for the Care of Victims of Torture, 2004).

24 Christina Boswell, *Spreading the Cost of Asylum Seekers: A Critical Assessment of Dispersal Policies in Germany and the UK* (York, Anglo Germany Foundation for the Study of Industrial Society, 2001).

25 Martin Bright, 'Refugees find no welcome in city of hate', *Observer,* 29 June 2003.

26 Human Rights Watch, *World Report* (Washington, DC, Human Rights Watch, 2002).

27 British Medical Association and Medical Foundation for the Care of the Victims of Torture, *Asylum Seekers and Health: A Dossier* (London, BMA, 2001).

28 Ibid.

29 British Medical Association, *Asylum Seekers: Meeting Their Healthcare Needs* (London, BMA Board of Science and Education, 2002).

30 Figure from *Older Refugees in Europe: Survey Results & Key Approaches,* ECRE Asylkoordination Osterreich, December 2002.

31 C. Timmis, 'Port in a storm: how Dover took asylum to its heart' *Law Gazette* (2006).

32 BBC Action Network, 'Understanding the asylum process', www.bbc.co.uk/dna/ican/A2151686 (accessed 13 October 2007).

33 Medical Foundation for the Care of Victims of Torture, www.torturecare.org.uk/publications/reports/277.

===

CHAPTER SIX

Asylum-seeking and Refugee Children: A Special Case

CHILDREN represent more than 50 per cent of the world's refugees and asylum seekers. Over the past ten years more than two million children have been killed in conflict, six million have been wounded and one million orphaned. In the UK children account for at least a quarter of those seeking asylum.[1] While there are no official figures, it is estimated that there are approximately 99,000 asylum-seeking and refugee children of compulsory school age living in the UK.[2]

It is something of a paradox that while children's education, health and welfare issues are uppermost on the social policy agenda, refugee children are left out of the picture, seen first as refugees and only second as children. National immigration laws and poorly coordinated services combine to put the mental health and welfare of refugee children at serious risk.

Most asylum-seeking and refugee children enter the UK with their families, and the first half of this chapter considers their experiences in the context of legal and social provision. In addition, a small but significant number arrive on their own. Known as unaccompanied or separated children, they share the predicament of other asylum-seeking and refugee children, but their situation makes them less visible and far more vulnerable.

JOAO'S STORY

Joao came with his mother, father and brother from Angola when he was six. He is now 22 and is on a business studies course in north London.

In Angola, we lived near the sea. We were always hungry, my mum says. There just never was enough food. She would have to walk twenty minutes each way to collect water everyday and I would have to do domestic chores before and after school.

My mum used to make cakes and sell them in the market and my father was a radio journalist. He got arrested after doing a story on some politicians and was tortured for three days. We left soon after that.

When we first came to Britain, everyone was nice to me and my brother. All I remember about coming was that we were at Heathrow and had to wait four hours to be interviewed. I was hungry and I went over to a lady who was eating and stretched out my hand. She gave me some of her food – but my mum shouted at me.

We still haven't been given leave to remain, which makes things difficult. I remember school trips, like skiing in France. I couldn't go because I had no legal status here. I felt so ashamed, I'd make up a story that I couldn't go because my mum was ill.

My parents split up two years ago and my dad is living in Birmingham with a new girlfriend and her two kids. My mum used to work at Kwik Save and as a school cleaner but she fell down the stairs and hurt herself badly, so now I buy all the food for the household. These days she sits in a room by herself a lot, reading the Bible.

I love England more than the country I came from. I'd like to see what Angola's like but this is my home.[3]

ASYLUM-SEEKING AND REFUGEE CHILDREN AND THE LAW

Children who have been granted refugee status or indefinite leave to remain (ILR) are entitled to the same provisions as children who are British citizens, such as access to education, health care and welfare benefits.[4] Those in the process of seeking asylum, however, are not; the entitlement to services such as benefits and health care is often determined by immigration status. The Government has ensured the permissibility of this policy by entering the Derogation on the UN Convention on the Rights of the Child, which means that the responsibility for providing care and support for unaccompanied asylum-seeking children lies firmly with local authorities' social services. Since the 1990s, following the arrival of children from Kosovo and Bosnia, local authorities have struggled to provide adequate care provision and, as a result, have been severely criticised.[5] The resultant pressure on funding has reinforced the perception that supporting unaccompanied children means higher council taxes and less money for 'deserving' vulnerable groups such as the elderly.[6]

Local authorities have responded to this criticism by pointing out that they are not given adequate funding to meet the needs of asylum-seeking children. Hillingdon Social Services for example point out that while the average council looks after 50 young asylum seekers, it has responsibility to care for around 1,140, due to its proximity to Heathrow. Consequently Hillingdon faces a financial crisis. Yet another difficulty is that the funding allocation is weighted towards younger children, whereas in practice they are outnumbered by older children, whose needs may be as complex.[7]

A key proposal of the Government's 2007 consultation document is to introduce policies which would deter children from coming to the UK. Those who did enter would be removed and returned to their country of origin on their eighteenth birthday.[8]

EDUCATION

The majority of refugee and asylum-seeking children attend schools in Greater London. It is estimated that in London one child in nineteen is a refugee, accounting for 6 per cent of all

children in the capital.[9] The largest number have come from
Somalia, Eritrea, Zimbabwe, Iraq, Iran and Afghanistan.[10]

Although officially all children of statutory school age in
the UK have a legal right to education, including those in
families seeking asylum, the reality is rather different. In a
survey carried out by the Refugee Council in July 2001, over
2,000 refugee and asylum-seeking children in London were
not in school, because they were either waiting to be relocated
or to be placed in permanent accommodation. Because local
schools and colleges will not admit students without a permanent address, which can take weeks and sometimes months to
organise, children's education is likely to be suspended during
that period.

There are further obstacles that these children face. In some
areas, particularly London, there is a shortage of school places.
In addition, few schools offer support in English language or
preparation classes and certain secondary schools are unwilling to admit refugee pupils for fear of their impact on GCSE
league tables. Finding a school for their children can therefore
be a confusing and demoralising scenario for refugee parents,
who are often unaware of their children's right to a school
place. And when they do manage to find a school, they face the
financial hardships of buying school uniforms and paying for
travel, school trips and other school-related expenses.[11]

But while some schools see them as a burden, others see
refugee and asylum seeker children as a positive asset to
the school and the community. Even pupils in areas predominantly hostile to asylum seekers have actively campaigned against the threatened deportation of fellow pupils.[12]
As one head teacher put it, 'The refugee children in this school
are an incredible resource for Britain. Some of them speak
four languages fluently. We should stop treating them as a
problem and tap into their valuable skills'.[13]

While the Government has suggested that child asylum
seekers be educated in special centres away from mainstream
schools, this view is by no means shared by organisations
concerned with the welfare of these children. A number,

including the British Medical Association, argue that to improve their integration into British society as well as their general well-being, they should be educated within the local community.[14]

The concern over their social exclusion is shared by the Children's Legal Centre at the University of Essex, which studied the current level of services received by refugee and asylum-seeking children.[15] They found that the procedures are so inconsistent that many children slip anonymously out of the system. The report urges the social inclusion of all refugee and asylum-seeking children living in Britain. If they are excluded as children, they will remain excluded and vulnerable for the rest of their lives.

ASYLUM AND REFUGEE CHILDREN IN DETENTION

Until 2001 refugee children were rarely detained in the UK. It is now estimated that 2,000 children each year – those in families as well as unaccompanied children – are held in detention, some for considerable periods of time.[16] Many families with children have been taken into detention with excessive force and intimidation, without being given an adequate explanation. In order to highlight this situation a number of organisations joined together in 2006 to form the 'No Place For A Child' campaign against the detention of children. One of the outspoken critics of these practices is no less a figure than HM Chief Inspector of Prisons, Anne Owers: 'The detention of children should be an exceptional measure and should not in any event exceed a very short period – no more than a matter of days.'[17]

It is known that detention can be very damaging to a child's mental and physical health. Research by the Bail for Immigration Detainees that looked at fifteen detained families found that the children suffered from a range of problems such as poor appetite, weight loss, listlessness, incontinence and disturbed sleep as well as anaemia, headaches, nosebleeds and anorexia.[18] One interviewee reported that children in one centre were sick and cried every night.

While the Government is committed to providing adequate on-site schooling to children in detention,[19] education in immigration detention centres – now known as removal centres – is invariably patchy and of inferior quality to that in mainstream schools. Because the numbers in detention are small, lessons take place for a limited number of hours each day and there is no obligation for the children to attend lessons. With uncertainty about how long they will be detained, there is little motivation to participate in the lessons.

> If they are released rather than deported after their detention, they may well not be able to go back to the area where they were previously at school. And even though they have done nothing wrong, they do not like to tell other children that they have just spent a couple of months in detention centres.[20]

Bill Bolloten, a refugee education consultant, further comments,

> This issue goes to the heart of the agenda around race equality and inclusion in education. At the moment there is a very strong agenda for schools to be responsive to the needs of all children and to be genuinely inclusive. If we have a situation where one group of children is not enjoying the same level of schooling and support that other groups of children enjoy in mainstream, then clearly we are looking at an issue of discriminatory treatment.[21]

Educating children in separate facilities has also caused disquiet in Parliament. In June 2002 MPs on the Joint Committee on Human Rights warned that the government's plans to extend the separate education of children in accommodation centres could have serious consequences. Their report concluded: 'Separate education on the basis of ethnicity or national origins breeds and entrenches social and educational inequality and inhibits or even deters integration.'[22]

Asylum-seeking children themselves are well aware of what this means in practice. After spending two years living in

Gravesend, Kent, where their four children attended the local schools, a Kurdish family were moved to Dungavel detention centre. The two older girls recalled their time in a mainstream school:

> Everyone accepted us and supported us, both pupils and teachers. We were very settled and the school made us feel at home. Now we don't have the opportunity to learn every subject and if the teacher is away or on holiday we don't have any lessons. We are learning things we already know and because all four of us learn together the standard is set at that of a seven year old who is the youngest.[23]

Offering separate educational provision within a context of detention has been described as educational apartheid. It is argued that the government should use the money to provide resources for child asylum seekers in mainstream school instead.[24]

PHYSICAL, EMOTIONAL AND MENTAL WELLBEING

More than a quarter of refugee and asylum seeker children in the UK have significant psychological difficulties, it is estimated, and many of their mental health needs are being left unmet.[25] In their short lives many of these children will already have experienced different types of traumatic events. For example, in their home country they may have witnessed violence and torture, seen a parent killed or the destruction of their home and livelihood, or been exposed to child labour. They may well have endured a horrendous journey in reaching their country of refuge – walking huge distances, becoming separated from their parents.

These children also face particular risks of sexual and gender-based violence including trafficking, child prostitution and abuse by persons with unrestricted access to them. At particular risk are unaccompanied and separated children, children in detention, former child soldiers, adolescents, mentally and physically disabled children, working children, teenage mothers, children born to rape victims/survivors, child perpetrators and those trafficked for prostitution.[26] Overall the reporting of child trafficking is increasing right across the UK.[27]

In the process of trying to integrate into a new country, new traumas may arise as a result of homelessness, destitution, bullying and racial harassment, including physical attack.[28]

UNACCOMPANIED ASYLUM-SEEKING AND REFUGEE CHILDREN

Every year over 2,500 unaccompanied children arrive in Britain, their nationalities reflecting hotbeds of unrest around the world. Unaccompanied children, sometimes referred to as unaccompanied minors, are defined as children under eighteen who have been separated from both parents, or orphaned, and who are not being cared for by an adult who, by law or custom, is responsible for them.[29] They may be with extended family members, in which case they are often referred to as 'separated children'. They may have been sent abroad by their parents or become victims of trafficking and/or the sex industry. A number of young refugees simply drop out of the system or disappear for what may be a variety of reasons, including trafficking for sexual or economic exploitation.[30]

The Refugee Council has set up a panel of advisors for unaccompanied children to provide support, assistance and advocacy. In addition, many local authorities have set up multi-agency forums to provide better services for these children. There is a very heavy demand on their services and priority is given based on need and urgency of individual cases.[31]

The psychological needs of the unaccompanied child may be immense. Child psychotherapist Sheila Melzak points out that unlike adult asylum seekers, the decision to flee has not usually been made by the unaccompanied or separated children themselves[32] and this fact may increase the child's feeling of powerlessness. Children who are traumatised because of witnessing atrocities committed against their parents or others may also face a range of ongoing emotional problems. Those working with these children report that their clients may present a range of problems including the difficulty of distinguishing between past and present experiences. Such children need to be helped so that the past, though not forgotten, does not continue to dominate the present.

> I came here by aeroplane from Africa, from Nairobi in Kenya. From the airport I came to London by train. A woman came with us. She took money from my family and she came with us. She had the passports and she did the talking. She answered when they asked questions at the airport. I don't know where she has gone now. Now I live with my uncle. My mother, she is in Nairobi. My dad died in Somalia, in the first day of the fighting. He fell on the floor and the soldiers captured him. My mum told me he was killed. When he was dead we went to Kenya. My mum wanted to go. We went to Nairobi in 1991 and spent four or five years there. But in Nairobi the police come and they check all the people to see if they have got passports. We left. Now I don't know how my mum is, or my brothers and sisters. (Ragi is a Somali boy who arrived in Britain in 1995 when he was ten years old.)[33]

AGE-DISPUTED ASYLUM-SEEKING AND REFUGEE CHILDREN

Verifying a child's age is important for two main reasons – to decide who is responsible for their care, and to establish what their rights are. Inevitably, many of the children have no documentation of any kind; they therefore cannot provide evidence of their date of birth. A number of unaccompanied children are sent to detention centres because immigration officers categorise them as adults due to their lack of documentation or their physical appearance.

Assessing the precise age of a child is difficult. A large number of unaccompanied minors are in the fourteen to

eighteen age range. The Royal College of Paediatrics and Child
Health accept that the margin of error for medical assessments
may be as much as five years.[34] Therefore a child of apparently
seventeen could be fifteen, seventeen or nineteen. While the
College recommends a holistic examination of the child, taking into account physical, mental, social and emotional development and maturity, the Home Office has not followed
this guidance. Immigration officers are advised to treat children as adults if their appearance strongly suggests they are
over eighteen (this being the age at which failed asylum seekers
can be removed from the UK). Almost half of asylum applications from unaccompanied children who are under eighteen are disputed by the immigration service. The figures are
even higher for Afghan children: of the 4,448 that arrived
between 2003 and 2006 and claimed asylum, almost 3,000 are
believed to have been age-disputed. This climate of disbelief
has been condemned by England's Children's Commissioner
Sir Albert Aynsley-Green:

> It's unacceptable that in too many of these cases the authori-
> ties fail to give young people the benefit of the doubt. I have
> been moved and angered by how children describe the dis-
> belief they often face – and how they fear the practical con-
> sequences of being treated inappropriately or as an adult. The
> stories they tell me are powerfully substantiated in this
> report.[35]

The Home Office is obliged to refer any person claiming to be
an unaccompanied minor to the Refugee Council's Panel of
Advisors, although at present only one in five children is
provided with a named advisor.[36]

There is also considerable confusion about what should
happen to unaccompanied children when they reach the age of
eighteen. Under the Children Leaving Care Act 2000, local
authorities have a duty to provide support for those leaving
care (care-leavers) as they move into adulthood, usually at
eighteen, and those in full-time education. They are expected
to treat them in the same way as a reasonable parent would,

which includes providing regular welfare check-ups and possibly paying for housing. However, the older a child is, the less money the local authority receives for them. Funding from central government is inadequate to help councils finance this work.[37]

LEVELS OF SUPPORT

Between July 2000 and February 2001 researchers at the charity Save the Children looked into the adequacy of support that unaccompanied children received. The researchers spoke to 125 young asylum seekers and refugees who had been separated from their parents or usual carers. They also spoke to 125 professionals working with these young people.

They found that the overall level of care and protection offered varied widely (a situation borne out by a subsequent survey of local authority provision across England in 2005).[38] A significant number [26] of the children interviewed had had chaotic and disturbing experiences on arrival and received little or no support. Young people aged sixteen and seventeen were found to be particularly disadvantaged: most who had arrived at that age were not looked after adequately and many were living in poor quality or inappropriate accommodation with little money. Some young people were living in unsupervised accommodation with adults, raising child protection concerns. Bullying and harassment had affected at least 30 per cent of those interviewed. The majority said they were physically healthy but many appeared to have emotional and possibly mental health problems.

However, in spite of these difficulties, the young people interviewed spoke of their desire to integrate into Britain, spend more time with their British peers and become economically independent to enable them to make a positive contribution to British society.

REMOVAL OF ASYLUM-SEEKING CHILDREN

Threat of removal is another anxiety facing unaccompanied refugee and asylum seeker children. Plans have been drafted by the Home Office to return unaccompanied young people to their home countries once they are eighteen, even to areas where war or ethnic violence remain rife.[39] The repatriation proposals could affect thousands of child refugees. The Home Office confirmed it plans to extend the scheme to all 24 countries on the 'white list' of safe countries, which includes Sri Lanka, Bangladesh, Serbia and Romania. The Refugee Children's Consortium, an umbrella group of, at the time of writing, 26 prominent charities, fears the Home Office is radically hardening its stance on young asylum seekers.

CONCLUSION

Both the data on the situation of unaccompanied children and the experiences of those working with them presents a disturbing picture. Several thousand children and young people are, to all intents and purposes, hidden from both public consciousness and from those support services which could help them. In the absence of a public consensus that unaccompanied children should receive support, and in the absence of a compassionate government policy towards them, many separated children are inadequately unsupported. This, compounded by overstretched and underfunded social services departments, a similarly overstretched voluntary sector, and the already impoverished refugee communities, results in too many of these children being left without proper care and support, leading to isolation, depression and poor nutrition.

Those working with these children are adamant that they should be entitled to all the welfare rights enshrined in the UN Convention on the Rights of the Child 1989 and have the same rights as children who are citizens. This means that all services should be developed so that asylum-seeking and refugee children are seen first and foremost as children: a vulnerable group in need of proper care and protection.

THE UNACCOMPANIED CHILD IN HISTORY

Unaccompanied refugee and asylum-seeking children in the twentieth century

Separated children have been coming to the UK and Europe throughout the twentieth century. In addition to Basque children who fled from the Spanish Civil War and Jewish children who fled from Nazi Germany (whose situation is discussed later in this chapter), groups of unaccompanied refugee children who arrived to the UK from the mid twentieth century include Hungarians during the uprising in 1956; Vietnamese among the boat people between 1975 and the late 1980s; those fleeing war in the former Yugoslavia from 1991 to 1994.

The Home Office started keeping records on unaccompanied children in 1992.[40] At that time there were about 200 unaccompanied children seeking asylum. The numbers have been increasing significantly over the last few years. Since 2003 the number of applications recorded from unaccompanied children has stayed broadly constant, at approximately 3000 per year.[41]

CASE STUDY 1: The Experience of Unaccompanied Spanish Refugee Children

In 1937 4,000 Spanish refugee children entered Britain in flight from the civil war in their country. Most of the children were aged between five and fifteen.

Among those who were against taking in the children were proponents of the view that a 'cold and Protestant England' wouldn't be good for them. Others argued that it would compromise the British government's policy of non-intervention if it appeared that they were siding with the Republican cause by taking in the Basque children.[42]

The bombing of Guernica in 1937 precipitated a change in government policy (as did Kristallnacht in Germany one year later). The Cabinet agreed to take some of the Basque children on the understanding that no cost would be borne by the British government and that the children would eventually be repatriated to Spain. The Home Office initially planned to limit the number to 2,000 but in the event about 4,000 refugee children came. A group known as the Basque Children's Committee was formed in May 1937 to organise the care and accommodation of these newly arrived refugees.

Inevitably, there was competition for places aboard the ships coming to Britain. Within a two-week period, between 10,000 and 20,000 children had signed up for the 4,000 available places. Britain was an attractive destination for the would-be refugees because of its historical connection with the Basque region.[43] Their arrival in Southampton was met with positive interest at both local and national level. The BBC was on hand to broadcast their disembarkation and a number of local people came to welcome them. Both the children and their parents initially thought they would be in Britain only for a few months. In fact a number stayed for two years, others stayed until the end of the second world war and a proportion of them remained indefinitely.[44] Notwithstanding the ambivalent voices, there was a generous response to these children among many, as evidenced in the number of people offering to take them into their homes. In addition, there were 90 'colonies' housing groups of children, many run by the Catholic Church.

When the Spanish Civil War ended in 1939 with victory for Franco, some 1,600 children remained in these colonies. Others lived in hostels for older children or with adoptive parents. Children over the age of fourteen were given the option of staying in Britain indefinitely. By the end of 1943 Home Office records showed that 411 of the evacuees still lived in Britain, most of them girls between the ages of fourteen and sixteen and boys aged eighteen to twenty. Both the former refugees and those who helped them look back on this period with some fondness, despite the mixed reception the children actually received:

> No other refugee group has received so much attention locally either at the time or subsequently in the public's imagination, but the privileged status of this story runs the risk of romanticism and nostalgia distorting the reality of the Basque experience in Britain which, for all its successes, had many difficulties. The Basque refugees were treated nationally and locally with sympathy, ambivalence and hostility. It was a complexity of responses that made it difficult for these often traumatised youngsters to re-establish a sense of home. Those fleeing persecution from the Third Reich faced similar dilemmas.[45]

CASE STUDY 2: The Experience of Unaccompanied Jewish Children (the Kindertransport)

The experience of the Kindertransport – the organised government-sponsored programme before the Second World War which allowed nearly 10,000 predominantly Jewish, unaccompanied children to come to Britain – is an excellent example of how government planning combined with public generosity resulted in a successful humanitarian programme.[46] This is not to say that there were no difficulties, but the fact remains that the children who came on the Kindertransport were spared from the death camps.

In November 1938 the House of Commons agreed to allow an unspecified number of children aged between three months and seventeen years to enter Britain, with a proviso that a £50 bond had to be posted for each child. The first of these transports left Germany six weeks after the infamous Kristallnacht (Night of the Broken Glass) pogroms, when the Nazis organised mobs to destroy synagogues and Jewish property and during which many Jews were harassed, beaten, arrested and killed.[47]

A total of 9,354 children made their way to Britain and were dispersed throughout the country. Half were taken in by foster families, both Jewish and non-Jewish, and the rest went to special hostels.[48] When the Second World War began, 1,000 of the older children were interned in the Isle of Man as 'enemy aliens', along with 19,000 other internees, about a third of whom were also refugees from Nazism. The irony of the situation was not lost on them. One detainee recalls:

> In Berlin I had a very long walk to and from school each day and frequently I was jeered and spat at when the German people realised I was Jewish. Now (in Douglas, on the Isle of Man), as we passed crowds of people, on either side we were jeered and spat at not because we were Jewish but because we were Germans.[49]

Within a relatively short space of time a number of the children from the Kindertransport had to face a second separation. This time it came in the form of evacuation to safe places outside the major cities. Inevitably, many of them were placed with families and communities that had never before seen a Jewish person. Many of the children eventually joined the British or Australian armed forces upon reaching the age of eighteen. Most never saw their parents again.

This fascinating chapter of both Jewish and British social history went relatively unrecognised for over forty years. It was only in the 1980s that people began to tell their stories of the Kindertransport.

BERTHA'S STORY

Bertha Leverton, née Engelhard, together with her brother Theo, was put on a Kindertransport train that took them from Munich to England on 4 January 1939. She was fifteen, he was eleven. She organised the first reunion of Kindertransport children fifty years later in London, to which 1,000 people came.

> My father heard through the grapevine about these trains that were taking Jewish children out of Germany. The times were getting worse and worse and he demanded from the Jewish

welfare office that they give him three places for his children. They said it was out of the question and would only give him two. Inge, aged eight, was left behind. My parents promised us that they would soon be coming. What we couldn't know then was that they would spend five years on the run through Europe, being smuggled across borders from Yugoslavia to Croatia to Spain and Portugal. They were allowed into Britain in 1940 thanks to a recently passed law permitting close relatives coming from neutral countries to enter the country if they had children under the age of fifteen here.

But in the meantime, Theo and I eventually arrived in Dovercourt in Kent, which was the reception camp for the Kinder, speaking not a word of English. Theo was designated foster parents first, a milkman's family in Coventry. I was sent to a plumber and his wife, also in Coventry. The milkman's children didn't like sharing with Theo so my childless 'family' – uncle Billy and aunty Vera – took him in.

My aim was to be the skivvy that they wanted and even though I point blank refused to wear a uniform, they showed me off, these working class people with a maid. They were awful but they agreed to take my sister Inge in after she came over on another Kindertransport that left on July 21st. War broke out on September 1st.

When the Blitz started, uncle Billy found a cottage in the countryside where we'd be safe. They'd take the three of us every evening during the bombings. One day, the people who rented the room asked who we were and uncle Billy told them we were Jewish children from Germany. They said 'oh, we don't want no Nazis here' so we had to stay in the centre of Coventry in a boarding house and go down to the cellar during the bombings. One time, our building took a direct hit. I was upstairs in the loo at that moment with my sister and everyone in the cellar assumed we'd been killed.

The fact is that my story is milder than most, though it was pretty rotten at the time. My parents survived: only 10 to 15 per cent of the Kindertransport children had their parents back again after the war.

NOTES

1 Mina Fazel and Alan Stein, 'Mental health of refugee children: comparative study', *British Medical Journal*, 327 (19 July 2003).

2 National Association for Language Development in the Curriculum, *Refugee and Asylum-seeker Children in UK Schools* (2004). See http://www.naldic. org.uk/ITTSEAL2/teaching/Refugeechildreninschool.cfm.

3 Private interview conducted by Reva Klein.

4 Judith Dennis, 'Only 3-5% of children receive either refugee status or discretionary leave to remain, compared with about 21% of adults', (London, Refugee Council, 2007).

5 'Minors conflict', *Guardian*, 31 January 2007.

6 Ibid.

7 Elli Free, *Local Authority Support for Unaccompanied Asylum Seeking Children*, (London, Save the Children, 2006).

8 Home Office, *Planning Better Outcomes and Support for Unaccompanied Asylum Seeking Children*, (2007). http://www.cnd.homeoffice.gov.uk/6353/ 6356/17715/uasc.pdfpp8.

9 Greater London Authority, *Offering More than They Borrow: Refugee Children in London*, (2004). http://www.london.gov.uk/mayor/refugees/doc/ refugee_children_report.rtf.

10 National Association for Language Development in the Curriculum, *Refugee and asylum-seeker children*. www.naldic.org.uk/ITTSEAL2/teaching/Refugee childreninschool.cfm, (accessed 13 October 2007).

11 Ibid.

12 Diane Taylor and Hugh Muir, 'Protests against decision to deport girl', (24 January 2005) http://education.guardian.co.uk/schools/story/0,5500, 1396949,00.html, (accessed 13 October 2007).

13 Tim Benson, Head Teacher, Nelson Primary School, East London, quoted in Alice O'Keeffe, 'Lost in Translation', *New Statesman* (February 2004).

14 British Medical Association, *Asylum-seekers: Meeting their Health Needs* (London, BMA, 2002).

15 *Mapping the Provision of Education and Social Services for Refugee and Asylum Seeker Children* (University of Essex, 2003). See http://www.childrenslegal centre.com/Templates/Internal.asp?NodeID=90361.

16 Lucy Krli, 'The impact of detention on a child's health and wellbeing', *Exile magazine*, issue 33, Refugee Council (September 2004).

17 'Dungavel, Inspectorate Calls for Limitations on Detention of Children' (HMIPS 042/ 2003), http://www.jcwi.org.uk/archives/ukpolicy/dungavel_ 14ang2003.pdf.

18 'Bail for immigration detainees – Quantitative research project on children in 15 detailed families' (November 2003), as reported in 'The impact of

detention on a child's health and wellbeing', Lucy Krli, *Exile magazine*, issue 33, Refugee Council, September 2004.

19   Anne Owers, Chief Inspector of Prisons, 'Introduction', *Report on Dungavel Removal Centre* (July 2002), as reported in 'Asylum, A Guide to Recent Legislation', *Immigration Law Practitioners Association* (January 2004).

20   Sarah Cutler, as quoted in Diane Taylor, 'Worlds Apart – Is it right for asylum-seeking children to be taken out of school and put in detention centres?', *Guardian*, 7 January, 2003.

21   Ibid.

22   As quoted in Diane Taylor, 'Worlds Apart – Is it right for asylum-seeking children to be taken out of school and put in detention centres?', *Guardian*, 7 January, 2003.

23   Ibid.

24   Eamonn O'Kane, General Secretary of the National Association of School-masters Union of Women Teachers, as reported in Taylor, 'Worlds Apart'.

25   Mina Fazel in *Newsletter of the University of Oxford*, vol. 4, issue 1, (9 October 2003).

26   M. Lay, I. Papadopoulos and A. Gebrehivot, 'Safer UK: Preventing Sexual Maltreatment of Unaccompanied Asylum-seeking Minors and Improving Services for Them', Research Centre for Trans-cultural Studies in Health, Middlesex University, 2007.

27   Christine Beddoe, ECPAT, 2006.

28   Fazel, *Newsletter of the University of Oxford*.

29   Within the European Union, basic figures on unaccompanied minors seeking asylum are not available from a number of countries, nor is there consistency in the way in which the statistics are kept. For example, in Germany the age limit for unaccompanied children is sixteen, compared to eighteen years as stipulated by the United Nations Convention on the Rights of the Child.

30   C. Beddoe, *Missing Out: A Study of child-trafficking in the North-West, North-East and West Midlands*, (UIC, 2007). Available from ECPAT UK or http://www.ecpat.org.uk/downloads/ECPAT_UK_Missing_Out_2007.pdf.

31   Judith Dennis, Refugee Council 2007.

32   Sheila Melzack is Principal Child Psychotherapist, Medical Foundation for the Care of Victims of Torture.

33   Hermione Harris, *The Somali Experience in the UK: What We Know and How We Know It*, (London, Information Centre about Asylum and Refugees in the UK, 2004).

34   Royal College of Paediatrics and Child Health, *The Health of Refugee Children – Guidelines for Paediatricians*, (London, The King's Fund).

35   'When is a Child not a Child?: Asylum, Age Disputes, and the Process of Age Assessment', Immigration Law Practioners Association, May 2007; see http://www.ilpa.org.uk/publications/ILPA%20Dispute%Report.pdf.

36 Children's Panel, (The Refugee Council, 2007).

37 'Minors conflict', *Guardian*, 31 January 2007.

38 Kate Stanley, *Cold Comfort: Young Separated Refugees in England*, (London, Save the Children, 2001).

39 Home Office, Planning Better Outcomes.

40 There are no statistics relating to separated children who do not come to the attention of the Refugee Council or who do not apply for asylum. According to the Refugee Council there are an unknown number of children who have been trafficked into the UK for some form of exploitation. These are known as 'undocumented' children. They have no immigration status and for all intents and purposes live a clandestine existence.

41 Home Office stats, http://www.homeoffice.co.uk/rds/pdfs07/asylumq107.pdf.

42 Tony Kushner & Katherine Knox, *Refugees in an Age of Genocide*, (London, Frank Cass, 1999), pp. 110–25.

43 Ibid.

44 Ibid.

45 Ibid, p. 125.

46 The exact figure is somewhat in dispute. According to the Institute of Contemporary History and Weiner Library the most authoritative account of the number of children who came during the Kindertransport is by Rebekka Gophert, *The Jewish Kindertransport from Germany to England – 1938/1939*. (Frankfurt, Campus, 1999). According to Gophert 9,354 children came from Germany to England of whom 90 per cent were Jewish. A Zionist organisation called Youth Aliyah brought over 700 children. The Union of Orthodox Hebrew Congregations brought over 100 Orthodox children. 154 children came from the Zbazsyn camp in Poland and a small group, the precise figure is not available, came from Czechoslovakia.

47 Each transport took between 100 and 600 children.

48 Ninety per cent of the children on the Kindertransport were Jewish, some were children of anti-Nazis or others singled out by the Nazis.

49 Herbert Levy, *Voices from the Past*, p.44, as quoted in Anne Karpf , *The War After*, (London, Minverva, 1996), p. 182.

CHAPTER SEVEN

Asylum, the Media and Public Opinion

> When you go out, you think about the media. You are not confident to face [those] people . . . and it creates a . . . sense of insecurity within you.[1]

THIS chapter focuses on the role of the media in shaping attitudes towards asylum and immigration attitudes. Of course, it is not the only influence; there are other significant factors. However, whether through our television sets, newspapers or hoardings, the mass media is pervasive and persuasive.

The press both reflects and reinforces public attitudes, thereby setting off a chain reaction in which reality is eventually buried under layers of myth and prejudice.[2] This symbiotic relationship between the media and public opinion, coupled with the ever-tightening succession of changes to asylum law, illustrates the extent to which the media, public opinion and government policy are intertwined.

There is nothing new in this. The tone and content of asylum and refugee issues follows a long-established pattern begun over 120 years ago when these topics first caused national controversy. The media's anti-asylum bias is in line with other moral panics created about vulnerable and voiceless groups, such as single mothers, but in recent years it appears to have intensified.[3] Over a ten-month period in 2000 the *Daily Mail* newspaper ran more than two hundred stories about asylum seekers – an average of one every other day.[4]

The historian Tony Kushner reports: 'The *Mail* has intensified its focus on the asylum seekers who are "swamping Britain" . . . in the six months preceding early March 2003, an electronic search came up with over 400 articles in the paper on asylum seekers, close to three items per day on average.'[5]

This relentless anti-asylum campaign was surpassed by the *Daily Express* which over the same period printed over six hundred articles on the subject.[6] Even the Council of Europe chastised the British media for their 'xenophobic and intolerant coverage of asylum issues'.[7]

People tend to read newspapers that reflect and reinforce their existing political bias.[8] Of the 12.5 million people who read daily newspapers, about 60 per cent read those tabloids which are in the main antagonistic towards asylum seekers. This means that about eight million people, around 12.5 per cent of the adult population of the UK,[9] are exposed on a fairly consistent basis to anti-asylum rhetoric.

The broadsheets are not completely innocent of anti-asylum sentiments either, judging by headlines that appeared in October 1997 such as 'Gypsies invade Dover' (*Independent*) and 'Tide of Gypsy asylum ebbs' (*Guardian*), although on the whole both these papers have dealt with the issues in a far more serious and analytical way than many of their Fleet Street counterparts.

The failure of the press to provide accurate, contextualised information about asylum issues can have an enormous impact on readers' perceptions, particularly when, as is usually the case, the distortions go unchallenged. Sensationalist headlines such as 'Asylum seekers steal the Queen's birds for barbecues',[10] or 'Illegal immigrants, asylum seekers . . . bootleggers . . . scum of the earth, drug smugglers . . . the back draft of a nation's human sewage',[11] reinforce a fear of asylum seekers by associating them with diseases such as HIV and TB, crime and terrorism. An editorial in the *Daily Mail* even called on its readers to stop donating money to the British Red Cross simply because the French Red Cross was running the Sangatte Asylum Centre.[12]

Photographs also play a major role in reinforcing damaging

images of asylum seekers. A study of the media coverage of the Red Cross centre Sangatte in France in 2003 showed that even though there were clear editorial differences on the subject between the various British papers, their visual messages were remarkably similar.[13] Over half the photographs showed un-named men in groups, confronting the French police, or with covered faces; there was no explanation as to why they might fear identification, and there were no pictures of the women and children in the camp. The study found that the impact of such imagery was greater than the content of any the articles, something that applies equally to television programmes.

The use of imagery in both photographs and cartoons contribute to what the researchers call 'the regular drip-feed of information that forms myths about the asylum issue'. They also point out that: 'The heavy editorialising of these images converted potentially inoffensive, or even heartening, photo-graphs into tools to communicate a very particular message to the reader; refugees and asylum seekers are undeserving re-cipients of better treatment than the average British citizen.'[14]

Cartoons, too, also perpetuate negative myths about as-ylum seekers. They are particularly powerful because they are precisely the sort of material which may be re-told in con-versation or passed around a group of friends, family, co-workers simply because of its 'amusement value'. In this interaction which allows it to seep much more easily into the collective consciousness it also legitimises what would norm-ally be considered to be socially unacceptable behaviour – to ridicule and demean a vulnerable group.[15]

RESEARCH INTO MEDIA COVERAGE OF ASYLUM ISSUES

The research project conducted in 2003 sheds light not only on the relationship between media coverage and asylum seekers but also on the extent to which asylum seekers and refugees themselves feel able to participate in the public debate on asylum and immigration and how media coverage can affect their everyday lives.[16] It was unusual in that it directly involved asylum seekers and refugees as researchers and as interviewees. Its main findings were:

1. Media reporting of the asylum issue is characterised by inaccurate and provocative use of language. Fifty-one different labels were identified as references to individuals seeking refuge in Britain and included meaningless and derogatory terms such as 'illegal refugee' and 'asylum cheat'.

2. Media reporting, particularly in the tabloid press, consistently fails to correctly distinguish between economic migrants and asylum seekers or refugees.

3. The asylum debate focuses overwhelmingly on the number of people entering the country to claim asylum, but figures presented in print and broadcast reports are frequently unsourced, exaggerated or inadequately explained.

4. Images used are dominated by the stereotype of the 'threatening young male'. Women and children are rarely seen and stock images of groups of men trying to break into Britain are used repeatedly.

5. News and feature articles on asylum rely heavily on politicians, official figures and the police as sources of information and explanation.

6. Asylum seekers and refugees feel alienated, ashamed and sometimes threatened as a result of overwhelmingly negative media coverage. Many of the interviewees reported direct experience of prejudice, abuse or aggression from neighbours and service providers. They attributed this to the way in which the media informs public opinion.

7. Many (asylum seekers and refugees) feel obligated to speak out about human rights abuses in their own countries and counter the myths about refugees in the UK.

The results of this study did not leave the researchers totally pessimistic. Improvements, they argue, could come about if politicians, government officials, reporters and editors worked more closely with refugee organisations to ensure that asylum seekers and refugee voices were clearly heard. However, given the entrenched attitudes of certain sections of the press, such a change in behavior is unrealistic. The *Guardian* journalist Roy Greenslade remarked that, on the whole, editors ignore the 'soft guidelines' on how to report asylum stories and that their behaviour is driven by both cynicism and commercialism.[17]

The researchers made a number of recommendations involving politicians, the press and refugees themselves. They suggest that politicians and government officials should take the lead in using accurate terminology when speaking about asylum and immigration;[18] that the Press Complaints Commission should develop 'soft guidelines' on reporting these issues; that the Home Office should explain statistics more clearly; and that the media should portray asylum seekers and refugees in less stereotypical ways – for instance by using more images of women, children and elderly people in their reports.

In addition, refugees and asylum seekers should be asked for their opinion on policy issues, giving them the opportunity to contribute to the asylum debate. These tasks could be made easier if exiled journalists were recruited who, in addition to their professional experience, could provide specific insight into issues relating to their countries.[19]

EFFECT ON PUBLIC OPINION

Britain's £1 billion asylum bill

> That's . . . enough to build up to TEN 450-bed hospitals . . . It could also pay for 150,000 new teachers, 40,000 beat police officers or 80 secondary schools.[20]

The powerful influence the media can exert on public perceptions has been demonstrated by The Glasgow Media Group[21]. In their work on attitudes to migration they found that audiences associated images of 'boat people'[22] and other migrants with political messages about the scarcity of resources in health and education.

The Information Centre about Asylum and Refugees in the UK investigated the role of information in creating understanding between local people and asylum seekers where a significant number of asylum seekers had moved or would be moving into an area for the first time.[23] In the absence of basic information, local people drew their own conclusions about the new arrivals, based on media myths about predatory males threatening their wives and daughters and economic migrants coming to Britain to sponge off the welfare state. The researchers concluded that 'there was a strong feeling amongst those interviewed that the national press serves to hinder understanding rather than promote it'.[24] But even though most of the interviewees criticised some of the tabloids for being inflammatory, they nevertheless accepted many of the myths they promoted.

Yet often, even where information is available, prejudice prevails. This was demonstrated by an analysis of the BBC television programme 'You the Judge', broadcast on Asylum Day 2003. Four real-life cases were presented to the studio audience, who were invited to adjudicate on them. Two of the cases had been dismissed by the Home Office. One of the remaining claimants had been granted Indefinite Leave to Remain on humanitarian grounds and the other had initially been rejected but was subsequently granted refugee status on appeal. The studio audience and the phone-in audience voted to reject the asylum seekers in all four cases. Ironically, the administration of 'justice' at the hands of the British public was even more stringent than that of the Home Office.

PUBLIC OPINION SURVEYS

What do public opinion surveys tell us about how the general public feels about asylum seekers and refugees?

One of the most significant findings of recent polls is that public attitudes to immigration and asylum issues are becoming increasingly negative. A poll conducted by MORI in the 1990s found that 5 per cent of the public felt that asylum and immigration issues were important. By December 2000 this figure had risen to 23 per cent and in February 2003 to 34 per cent.[25] In the same year a poll for *The Times* found that nine out of ten voters felt that asylum seekers in the country were a serious problem and 39 per cent felt that the number of asylum seekers was in fact 'the most serious problem facing Britain today'.[26] By 2005 race relations, immigration and immigrants ranked as the single most important issue in the minds of the public.[27]

It is common for people to overestimate both the number of asylum seekers in the country and the actual level of support they receive.[28] A Reader's Digest poll (2002) found that respondents believed that the UK hosted 23 per cent of the world's refugees (the actual figure was under 2 per cent) and that asylum seekers were given £113 a week (the actual figure was £36.54).[29]

Commenting on these findings Russell Twisk, the editor in chief of *Reader's Digest*, wrote,

> This widespread resentment of immigrants and asylum seekers has worrying implications in a society that has traditionally prided itself on its racial tolerance. Do these attitudes reveal a deep-seated xenophobia or are they fuelled by segments of the media that can be accused of turning a normal trend in to a perceived crisis?[30]

The 2005 IPPR study found that young people were the most polarised group, expressing at one end of the spectrum extreme hostility to asylum seekers and at the other end a strong belief that the UK should welcome them.[31] This bears out previous research. A 2002 survey of fifteen to eighteen-year-olds found that 31 per cent believed that almost one third of the world's refugees lived in Britain. Only 19 per cent felt that Britain ought to be welcoming to asylum seekers, compared to 26 per cent of adult respondents.[32] Another poll the

following year of fifteen to 24-year-olds reported that a significant number of young people in Britain had negative views
on asylum seekers and were ill informed.[33] Fifty-eight per cent
felt that asylum seekers and refugees did not make a positive
contribution to the UK. Twenty-three per cent thought that
Britain should not offer a safe haven to people fleeing war or
persecution. Under half (48 per cent) believed that few asylum
seekers are actually genuine.

At the same time 57 per cent of those interviewed felt that
Britain should offer protection to those in need and over half
felt that asylum seekers had a right to education and to
employment.[34] More encouragingly, another poll in Northern
Ireland in 2005 found generally positive attitudes among
young people, except among a 'significant minority'. (As with
adult respondents, young people also misunderstood the
reasons why refugees had come to the UK.)[35] Similarly,
MORI (2003) found that 78 per cent of the adult population
felt that 'it is right that Britain should continue to let in people
seeking asylum if their claim is genuine.'[36] This latest figure is
consistent with opinion polls carried out since 1977.

Another measure of public opinion in the UK can be found
in both the 2004 European and local elections, and in the 2005
General Election. The increase in support for both the BNP
(British National Party) and UKIP (United Kingdom Independence Party), with their explicitly anti-asylum message,
reveals a worrying trend.[37]

What informs public opinion? Press coverage certainly
plays a pivotal role in fuelling myths and rumours about
asylum seekers: thanks to distortions in the popular press, for
instance, there is a widespread belief that asylum seekers
receive disproportionately generous benefits, including free
bus passes and free swimming and driving lessons.[38]

> The drip, drip, drip of negative stories and alarmist headlines
> in papers that command the attention of a huge swathe of the
> adult British population cannot but have a negative impact on
> public opinion. If the only information provided to readers is

hostile, one-sided, lacking in context and often wildly inaccurate, how can they be expected to see through the distorted
media narrative?[39]

How do the national media interact with other factors? One
of the main conclusions of the IPPR report was that the
media has a complex relationship with public opinion, but
that they do not necessarily influence an individual's views.
Local papers are more trusted and therefore far more influen-
tial than the national press. Even more significant, though,
is what politicians do and say and how they say it.[40] Their
behaviour sets the tone for what is subsequently reported in
the media.[41]

Another major factor is where people get their information
from. According to this research, around 33 per cent rely on
friends, family and neighbours (who, in turn, rely on other
friends, family and neighbours). Thirty-eight per cent get their
information from what they see around them, or think they
see (asylum seekers are often confused with members of settled
ethnic minorities). This is worrying because 'personal experience is difficult to challenge and these kinds of interactions are
powerful, reinforcing prejudice within others'.[42]

Opportunities for meaningful, as opposed to superficial
contact with asylum seekers and ethnic minority communities
also play an important part: the most hostile views are found
in areas with fewest asylum seekers. Paradoxically, an ethnically diverse city such as Birmingham offers fewer opportunities for meaningful contact because its various communities
are quite segregated. By contrast, more positive attitudes
towards asylum seekers are found in areas such as Camden
in North London, where communities are far less separate
from each other in terms of housing and schooling and people
from different communities meet as parents, neighbours and
friends. These findings are supported by a MORI poll (2003)
which found that 75 per cent of people in London thought that
living in a multi-cultural society was a good thing.[43]

The extent to which people believe their public services

are under threat because of asylum seekers is another important factor in determining attitudes.[44] Other variables including age, socio-economic status, educational level and ethnic
background, feed into a complex range of views. For example,
while middle-class people aged between 25 and 50 are the
most tolerant towards asylum seekers, those with university
degrees have recently shown the greatest increase in hostility
of any group. Settled ethnic minority communities are relatively well informed about refugees and concerned about
human rights; at the same time they are afraid of being
confused with asylum seekers and see them as a potential
economic threat.[45]

What accounts for the dichotomy in public opinion?[46]
Three possible answers suggest themselves. The belief that the
UK has always been a haven for refugees may still resonate in
the public consciousness. The tension between a collective
sense of fairness – supposedly part and parcel of being British
– and the constant negativity surrounding the issue, might be
a contributory factor. Finally, the increase in asylum applications throughout the 1990s coincided with a period of
rapid social change on many fronts, playing into fears about
loss of national identity. An example of these paradoxical
views was seen during the campaign to win the Olympic bid
for London: the cosmopolitan nature of the city was promoted
as a major selling point while at the same time a negative
debate was taking place about eastern European workers
flooding Britain's labour market.[47]

CASE STUDY 1: Articles about Sangatte Asylum Centre

Few stories about asylum have attracted as much media attention as those generated from the Sangatte asylum centre. A
former warehouse, Sangatte, opened in September 1999 as a
shelter to house asylum seekers who had been sleeping rough
in and around Calais. It came to international notice in 2001
when hundreds of asylum seekers from the centre, most of
them Kurds, Iraqis and Afghanis, attempted to enter the UK

illegally via the Channel Tunnel and Eurostar trains. Informed by the organised smugglers who had arranged their journeys to Europe that the only way they could enter Britain was by avoiding detection, they risked life and limb to make it across the Channel, some of them repeatedly. Their determination not to stay in France was guided by a number of factors, including, for a number of them, the desire to be reunited with family members in Britain. Some were reluctant to stay in France because they spoke English but no French and for others, it was Britain's reputation for 'tolerance' of asylum seekers. The British government's response was to strike a deal with the French in which 1,200 of the nearly 5,000 inside Sangatte were allowed to come to the UK, where they were issued with four-year work permits and helped to find jobs. The others were given asylum by the French authorities. The Sangatte episode led to a tightening of immigration controls at Channel ports and Britain's establishment of full border controls in France.[48]

Over a three month period leading to the camp's closure, this was the most frequently reported story relating to asylum and immigration.[49] The coverage encompassed the whole range of anti-refugee rhetoric, ranging from relative silence (*Daily Telegraph*, *Daily Mirror*) to intense focus (*Daily Mail*, *Daily Express*); and from neutral reporting (*Guardian*) to extreme prejudice (*Daily Mail*, *Daily Express*, *Sun*).[50]

The *Mail* and the *Express* matched each other in coverage of the story, each producing 21 articles on the issue. They reiterated the message that the inhabitants of the Sangatte camp were untrustworthy and that the impending arrival of an unknown, and allegedly 'massive' number of them in the UK was cause for great concern.[51] The labels – 'bogus' 'parasites' and 'scroungers' – were used repeatedly to describe those living in Sangatte, thus continuously reinforcing the notion that these people were, in fact, nothing more than cheats. Not only were they undesirable, they would be a drain on both the British taxpayer and public services and a threat to the nation's security. The researchers also found that television coverage did little to correct this media imbalance as programmes associated these asylum seekers/refugees by implication with terrorism, war and danger.[52]

In contrast to this negative reporting, research for the Red Cross presented a different story: 'Britain's view that the controversial Sangatte refugee camp acts as a global magnet for would-be illegal immigrants to Britain is "profoundly ill-informed" and bears no relation to the experience of the thousands of refugees who pass through it'.[53] Their analysis showed that only a small minority of the camp's mainly Kurdish and Afghan inhabitants were actually planning to try to reach Britain when they first left their home countries, and that only a few knew Sangatte existed before they reached western Europe. 'The idea that it is Sangatte that attracts the refugees reveals a huge historical and sociological misunder-standing not only of the reasons why people leave their homes, but of the conditions that precede their departure. It also reveals ignorance of what it means to illegally cross coun-tries.'[54]

The Red Cross report also revealed the human side of asylum:

> The decision to leave is usually taken by the whole family, which explained why so few would-be immigrants gave up en route. Fathers and uncles sold everything to finance the jour-ney, usually designating the family's youngest and fittest adult male and charging him with the 'mission' of escaping and making good abroad. It's not the oldest or the poorest who leave. People flee to pick up again what has been halted or banned in their country: an education, a business, a profes-sion, a good school for their children. And you need a body in working order, and the dreams of youth.[55]

The research into media coverage of asylum sheds a harsh light on the massive discrepancies between reality on the ground and how the popular press presents the issues. Stories that might humanise asylum seekers by telling their personal stories are few and far between: by dehumanising this very disparate group of people, the media is more able to vilify them.

CASE STUDY 2: Articles about Asylum Seekers Eating Swans and Donkeys

The Refugees, Asylum Seekers and the Media (RAM) Project highlighted the extraordinary story of how the *Sun* newspaper (circulation 3.5 million daily) wrote an exclusive, though unfounded, front-page story: 'Callous asylum seekers are barbecuing the Queen's swans'. *Sun* readers were told that 'East European poachers lured the protected royal birds into baited traps'. They also reported that, according to an official Metropolitan Police report, 'the asylum seekers were barbecuing a duck in a park in Beckton, East London. But two dead swans were also found concealed in bags and were ready to be roasted. The discovery last weekend confirmed fears that immigrants are regularly scoffing the queen's birds'.[56]

By good fortune, a communications officer at the RAM project (who happened to be an exiled journalist from East Europe) was suspicious about this story. He subsequently contacted three local police stations and found that there was no record of this alleged offence. It was discovered that the story was based on unsubstantiated allegations made by unnamed members of the public. The *Sun* finally had to accept that it was impossible to substantiate the allegation. The incident was reported to the Press Complaints Commission. Consequently, the Sun was told to produce a disclaimer stating that they had confused conjecture with fact – five months after the story first appeared.

Not to be outdone, the *Daily Star* produced yet another dubious story one month later (August 2003), this time about asylum seekers eating donkeys.[57] Again using conjecture rather than fact, this popular tabloid chose to use unfounded sensationalist headlines to demonise and criminalise refugees. In this case they blamed Somali refugees for stealing donkeys from Greenwich Royal Park, an ironic choice as most Somalis in fact do not eat meat of any kind.

The ease with which both the swan and the donkey stories made their way into the headlines should ring alarm bells and raise questions about how capable the press is of policing itself given the fact that since 1990 journalists have been required to abide by an ethical code of practice which was in fact drawn up by newspaper editors themselves.[58]

The very first clause of this code states that newspapers and periodicals must take care not to publish inaccurate, misleading or distorted material.[59] These stories also breached Clause 13 of the code that states that newspapers must avoid prejudicial or pejorative reference to a person's race, colour or religion.[60]

CAMPAIGN TO ALTER PUBLIC OPINION

Use of Advertising

In 1997 the Refugee Council commissioned a public relations company to plan a campaign to alter public attitudes towards refugees.[61] The underlying research found that refugees were so marginal to people's lives that they found it hard to identify with them. Refugees were not seen as a cause with the same status as, say, world poverty. Any existing sympathy towards them was diminished if Britain was criticised for its treatment of refugees. Often-used arguments such as the contribution refugees make to British life did nothing to engender more sympathetic views. Statistics demonstrating the relatively small number of refugees in Britain made no impact either. The researchers did find, however, that talking about refugees as 'ordinary people in extraordinary circumstances' and thinking about them not as objects of charity but as people 'just like you and me' made identification easier. They concluded that a move from 'superficial sympathy' to 'empowered empathy' would encourage more positive identification. This, in turn, would help develop more enlightened attitudes towards refugees and asylum seekers. It has yet to be seen whether advertising can be used as an effective tool in this process.

Refugee Week

This is an initiative of the Refugee Council, which began in 1999. Its aim is to 'celebrate the enormous economic and cultural contribution of refugees and asylum seekers to the UK and promote understanding about the reasons why people seek sanctuary – through arts, cultural and educational events that take place all over the UK'.[62] Thousands of people take part in this festival annually in mainstream venues as well as in educational institutions and youth groups with over 300 public events, offering a range of cultural, social and political events. The effect these events have on influencing public opinion is yet to be determined.

THE IMPACT OF MYTHS ON REFUGEES AND ASYLUM SEEKERS THEMSELVES

It is difficult to determine what impact negative media coverage has on refugees and asylum seekers themselves. The Article 19 study attempted to analyse this by interviewing a number of asylum seekers.[63] They found that the interviewees felt deep frustration because of the way the media portrays them as a single homogeneous group, ignoring the fact that asylum seekers and refugees come from many different parts of the world, and that each have their own reasons for leaving their countries as well as their individual histories and attachments.

Frustration was also felt because of the way the media reinforces the notion that all asylum seekers are fleeing from poverty, ignoring the fact that many asylum seekers and refugees were actually middle-class, well-educated professionals in their countries of origin. Research carried out by the Institute of Public Policy Research (IPPR) concluded that 'there is little or no empirical evidence that welfare support is a principle motivation for choosing to come to the UK. Few asylum seekers are fully aware of what benefits are available to them on their arrival, nor do they have a good knowledge of the differences between asylum determination processes in different countries.'[64]

However, in spite of some positive views presented in the media the overall conclusion of the report was that, 'the testimonies of those asylum seekers interviewed confirmed that the provocative and inaccurate coverage of the asylum issue had direct and at times distressing consequences for asylum seekers and refugees living in this country.' Consequently, it is the people – not the policy – that become the target of public resentment,[65] making them more vulnerable to racial attacks. It is estimated that there were over 2,000 attacks on dispersed asylum seekers during a recent two-year period. Violence against asylum seekers has become such a concern that the Association of Chief Police Officers (ACPO) commented that 'racist expressions towards asylum seekers appear to have become common currency and acceptable in a way which would never be tolerated towards any other minority.'[66] The fear of physical attack is not only felt by refugees and asylum seekers but also by people working with them. 'If organisations feel intimidated by the press in this way, it is not surprising that individual refugees and asylum seekers tend to feel even more powerless.'[67]

Powerlessness is also a theme in research carried out by the Information Centre about Asylum and Refugees in the UK (ICAR). The researchers were interested in examining ways to manage the arrival of asylum seekers into different local communities across the UK in such a way that tension, on the part of both local people and asylum seekers, could be reduced.

The research focused on six centres: Bicester, Dover, Leeds, Leicester, Newcastle and Oakington. They discovered that in these areas local people and asylum seekers were strangers to each other, thereby fuelling each group's anxiety about the other. This, in turn, perpetuated the spread of myths and rumours. Anxieties of this kind could be reduced by producing a 'tool kit' which could be used to encourage local people and asylum seekers to meet each other and which would provide adequate resources and information networks. A strategy combining information and activities could help alleviate tensions as well as speed up the successful 'integration' of asylum seekers into local areas.

One of the most successful examples of asylum seekers being positively received into a community is the experience of Kosovan refugees arriving in Leeds in 1999. Much preparatory work was done with the press and local community before the arrival of the refugees. Unfortunately, the experience of Kosovans in Leeds is atypical.

This chapter has focused on the powerful impact the media have on creating and sustaining anti-refugee sentiments. Such sentiments have become part of conventional wisdom, becoming integrated into the public's collective thinking. The government's behaviour towards asylum seekers and refugees, both in terms of implementing harsh asylum legislation and its ambiguous attitudes towards them, reinforces negative atittudes. Since the government offers little opposition to the demonisation of refugees, the whole process becomes institutionalised.

New ways of rehabilitating the very concept of asylum and refuge need to be found. Community involvement as demonstrated both by the experience of Kosovan refugees coming to Leeds and the grass roots work carried out by organisations such as ICAR, are eminently useful models.

FARRAH JUDY'S STORY

Farrah Judy is a Lebanese mother of three married to a Palestinian. A qualified physiotherapist, she and her family have been living in London for eight years.

> I come from a well off Lebanese family. We had a large house with a garden, orchards, fig trees and grape vines. I earned good money as a private physiotherapist.
>
> When I married, I moved into the refugee camp near Saida

with my husband, since he wasn't allowed to live outside the camp. My two children born there are stateless like my husband because they are Palestinian. Instead of a passport, they have a UN ticket. By law, you're not allowed to work outside the camp. There are 75 different professions represented in that camp and they're all living on their wits, servicing and looking after each other.

Our family was in danger in the camp, which is why we came here claiming asylum. On 23 October 2003, we lost our asylum appeal. And then on the 25th, there was an amnesty of all people whose appeals had been rejected.

We've lived in many temporary flats and bed and breakfast hotels since coming to London. All were small, a couple were not safe for children. But they were not bad except for the flat we have now in Westbourne Grove. Lots of children around the estate smoke drugs and I don't allow my children to play outside.

The government is paying us housing benefit for this temporary accommodation because we're still not allowed to work. It would be so much better to let us work and let us live in permanent housing. These rules and laws are not logical, they don't make sense.

I have more English friends now than Arab friends. They're honest with me. We're different in religion but not in our humanity. I know that it's not shameful to be a refugee and it's not better to be English than a Palestinian. I want my children to respect their identities – half Palestinian, half Lebanese, half Sunni, half Shia – and to respect English people when they deserve that respect. I want peace for my family and an environment that protects our beliefs. I want there to be honest judgment on what happens in the world. When there's a bomb somewhere, I don't want to go out and have someone look at me with hatred or suspicion.

NOTES

1 A community activist from Bhutan interviewed in Leeds by Sara Buchan, Bethan Crillo and Terry Threadgold, for *What's the story? Media Representation of Refugees and Asylum Seekers in the UK*, (London, Article 19, 2003).

2 Roy Greenslade, *Seeking Scapegoats – The Coverage of Asylum in the UK Press, Asylum and Migration Working Paper 5* (London, IPPR, 2005), p. 6.

3 The term 'moral panic' was coined by sociologist Stanley Cohen in 1972 in his book *Folk Devils and Moral Panics.*.

4 Tim Bouquet and Devid Moller, 'Are we a tolerant nation?' *Readers Digest* (November 2000) as quoted by Tony Kushner in 'Meaning nothing but good: ethics, history and asylum-seeker phobia in Britain', *Patterns of Prejudice, vol. 37, No. 3,* (2003) p. 257.

5 Ibid., p. 28.

6 Ibid., p. 258.

7 Ian Black, 'UK most racist in Europe on refugees', *Guardian,* 3 April 2001. Further criticism on UK's media appears in the Council of Europe's Parliamentary Assembly document 10280 (20 September 2004).

8 Miranda Lewis, *Asylum – Understanding Public Attitudes* (London, IPPR, 2005), p. 23.

9 Greenslade, *Seeking Scapegoats,* p. 6. As it is estimated that three people read every bought copy of a newspaper, Roy Greenslade points out that this would result in more than 22 million people reading the four newspapers which are the most critical of asylum seekers. This represents more than a third of the entire British population.

10 *Sun,* 4 July 2003.

11 *Dover Express,* 1 October 1998.

12 *Daily Mail* 'A Cause unworthy of your support', 17 May 2002.

13 Buchanan, Grillo and Threadgold, *What's the Story?*

14 Ibid., p. 25.

15 Ibid., p. 27.

16 Ibid.

17 Roy Greenslade speaking at Refugee Council AGM (February 2004).

18 The juxtaposition of these two headlines in *The Times,* 14 February 2001 is typical of this: 'Illegal workers imported by Mafia' next to 'Asylum-seekers are exploiting rights charter'. The interchange and juxtaposition of 'illegal immigrant' with 'asylum seekers' throws an air of illegality over all asylum seekers, while mistrust and suspicion are generated by constant references to 'bogus asylum seekers'. Contrary to popular terminology, there can in fact be no such thing as a 'bogus asylum seeker' (evidence for *claims* for asylum might be unavailable, or even false in some cases, but a person claiming asylum can *only* be a genuine asylum seeker). This distinction seems lost even on Tony Blair, who said on 1 March 2000 'Those measures will help us separate bogus asylum seekers from genuine asylum seekers.'

19 Ibid.

20 *News of the World,* 19 May 2002, quoted in Greenslade, *Seeking Scapegoats,* p. 22.

21 The Glasgow Media Group is part of the Department of Sociology,

Anthropology and Applied Social Sciences at Glasgow University. The Unit has developed techniques to link the analysis of media content with the processes by which audiences receive and interpret messages.

22 Refugees who fled Vietnam in small boats in the late 1970s.

23 Lisa D'Onofrio and Karen Munk, *Understanding the Stranger,* interim case study findings commissioned and published by ICAR, July 2003. Quoted in Buchanan, Grillo and Threadgold, *What's in the Story: results into media coverage of refugees and asylum seekers in the UK,* Article 19, p. 13.

24 Ibid.

25 MORI 'British Views on Immigration' (February 2003) in Matt Gill and Heaven Crawley, *Asylum in the UK, an IPPR Fact File* (London Institute for Public Policy Research, 2003).

26 Populous Poll, *The Times,* February 2003.

27 MORI 2005.

28 Readers Digest poll, in IPPR, ibid. (November 2005).

29 Gill and Crawley, *Asylum in the UK,* p. 37.

30 Ibid., footnote 20.

31 Ibid., Miranda Lewis, 'Asylum: Understanding Public Attitudes', Institute for Public Policy Research, 2005.

32 MORI, Social Research Institute for Refugee Week (June 2002).

33 MORI, 'British views on immigration' (London, MORI, 2003).

34 Ibid., Miranda Lewis. The IPPR (2005) found that the age group 17–19 had the most diverse attitudes on asylum seekers. Some expressed extreme levels of hostility and an equal number felt strongly that asylum seekers should be welcomed into the UK. The split was correlated with educational levels.

35 Amnesty International, Declan McKerr, *Refugees and Asylum Seekers: Northern Ireland Youth Attitudes Survey,* Belfast 2004.

36 MORI, 'British Views on Immigration'.

37 'UKIP makes big gains in Euro poll', http://news.bbc.co.uk/1/hi/uk_news/politics/3803505.stm; 'Kilroy: We'll wreck EU Parliament', http://news.bbc.co.uk/1/hi/uk_politics/3803599.stm; 'Election 2005', http://news.bbc.co.uk/1/hi/uk_politics/vote_2005/default.stm (all accessed 13 October 2007).

38 'Asylum: Understanding Public Attitudes', Miranda Lewis, Institute for Public Policy Research, 2005, p. 28.

39 'Seeking Scapegoats: The coverage of asylum in the UK press' (Roy Greenslade, Institute of Public Policy Research, June 2005), p. 29.

40 'Asylum: Understanding Public Attitudes', Miranda Lewis, Institute for Public Policy Research, 2005.

41 This view is supported by an evaluation of the British Attitude Survey (BSA) which found that it is the current framing of the political discourse that provides the best explanation for the negative increase in attitudes towards asylum seekers. (McLaren and Johnson, as reported in the IPPR Survey) p. 21, 2004.

42 Ibid. Miranda Lewis IPPR Survey: 'Understanding Public Attitudes', London (2005) p.15.

43 Ibid. (Article 19) also found that negative opinions were based on anxiety (generated by media coverage) rather than on personal experience of meeting refugees. People in both London and the South East, places thought of as experiencing the most strain because of the numbers of asylum seekers, had the most tolerant views about them.

44 Ibid. Here the IPPR also points to the absolute importance of the role of politicians in changing peoples' attitudes. The report concludes that unless attempts to address peoples' fears are met with political commitment to tackle inequality and injustice, then negative attitudes are likely to persist.

45 Ibid.

46 Ibid. Miranda Lewis, 'Asylum: Understanding Public Attitudes'. The IPPR survey also found that respondents' attitudes were both complex and contradictory.

47 Yasmin Alibhai-Brown at Black-Jewish Dialogue breakfast meeting, February 2004.

48 Under the European Union's 'safe third country' agreement, asylum seekers must ask for protection in the first 'safe' country they reach, when possible. This ruling is intended to put an end to asylum seekers choosing the country in which to seek refuge. Legally, the Sangatte asylum seekers should have claimed asylum in France or whatever the first 'safe' country was that they reached. How they would have been aware of this law is not clear.

49 Buchanan, Grillo and Threadgold, 'Appendix 2 – a case study of the media coverage of the closure of Sangatte' in *What's the Story?*

50 Ibid. The *Guardian* was the only newspaper to publish a background piece tracing the history of the Red Cross centre from its opening as a humanitarian shelter three years previously.

51 Ibid. Little mention was made of the fact that it was the French who bore the greatest responsibility for the people living in Sangatte as they took in over 3,600 asylum seekers, three times the number Britain allowed in.

52 Ibid.

53 Smain Laacher, quoted in John Henley, 'Britain ill informed about Sangatte', *Guardian*, 25 June 2002, http://politics.guardian.co.uk/homeaffairs/story/0,11026,743505,00.html (accessed 13 October 2007).

54 Ibid.

55 Ibid.

56 *Sun*, 'Swan Bake', 4 July 2003.

57 *Daily Star*, 'Asylum Seekers Eat our Donkeys', 21 August 2003.

58 Roy Greenslade, 'Dead Meat?', *Guardian*, 1 December 2003.

59 Ibid.

60 Ibid.

61 Rainey Kelly Campbell Roalfe, *Refugees – From a Small Issue to an Important*

Cause – Research Debrief (London, Refugee Council, 1997). It is worth noting that refugee issues were thought of as a small cause in 1997.

62 The Refugee Council Website, 2004.

63 Buchanan, Grillo and Threadgold, *What's the Story?*

64 Gill and Crawley, *Asylum in the UK*, p. 2.

65 Buchanan, Grillo and Threadgold '*The impact of myths on refugees and asylum seekers*' (2003) p. 41.

66 Association of Chief Police Officers, *Guide to Meeting the Policing Needs of Asylum Seekers and Refugees*, (London, ACPO, 2001).

67 Ibid., footnote 67, p. 42.

Further reading

Association of Chief Police Officers (February 2001) *Guide to Meeting the Policing Needs of Asylum Seekers and Refugees*

Alibhai-Brown, Y. (2000) *Who Do We Think We Are? – Imagining a New Britain*, (London, Penguin Books)

Ayotte, W. and Williamson, L. (2001) '*Who are Separated Children?*' in *Separated Children in the UK. An Overview of the Current Situation* (London, Refugee Council and Save The Children)

Blackwell, D. and Melzack, S. (2000) *Far from the Battle but Still at War – Troubled Refugee Children in Schools* (London, The Child Psychology Trust)

Buchanan, S., Grillo B. and Threadgold, T. (2003) *What's the Story? Media Representation of Refugees and Asylum Seekers in the UK* (London, Article 19)

Bouquet, T. and Moller, D. (November 2000) '*Are we a tolerant nation?*', *Readers Digest*, quoted by Tony Kushner in 'Meaning nothing but good: ethics, history and asylum-seeker phobia in Britain' and *Patterns of Prejudice*, vol. 37. no. 3

Gill, M. and Crawley, H. (2003) *British Views on Immigration, Asylum in the UK, an IPPR Fact File* (London, MORI)

Greenslade, R. (May 2005) *Seeking Scapegoats – The Coverage of Asylum in the UK Press – Asylum and Migration Working Paper 5* (London, IPPR)

ILPA (2004) *Asylum, A Guide to Recent Legislation* (Immigration Law Practitioners Association)

Karpf, A. (1996) *The War After* (London, Minerva)

Kushner, T. (2003) 'Meaning nothing but good: ethics, history and asylum-seeker phobia in Britain', in *Patterns of Prejudice*, vol. 37, No. 3

Kushner, T. and Knox, K. (1999) *Refugees in an Age of Genocide*, Chapter 4, 'Refugees from the Spanish Civil War' (London, Frank Cass), pp. 110–125

Lewis, M. (2005) *Asylum – Understanding Public Attitudes* (London, IPPR)

London, L. (2000) *Whitehall and the Jews 1933–1948, British Immigration Policy and the Holocaust* (Cambridge, Cambridge University Press)

Refugee Council (2006) *Older Refugees in the UK: A Literature Review. A Refugee Council Working Paper for the Older Refugees Programme.* (London, Refugee Council)

Sherlock, M. (June 2004) *Refugees: Renewing the Vision. An NGO Workpaper on Improving the Asylum System* (London, Refugee Council)

Sherman, A. J. (1973) *Island Refuge: Britain and the Refugees from the Third Reich 1933–1939* (London, Frank Cass)

Speers, T. (2001), 'Refugees and Asylum Seekers in the Welsh Press' in Keelin Howard, 'Is it a crime to seek refuge?', *Criminal Justice Matters*, 43

CHAPTER EIGHT

Conclusion

After the two catastrophic world wars of the last century, several genocides and the threat of nuclear annihilation, the start of the new millennium offered the possibility of renewed hope. Today, this optimism appears a million miles away from the disappointment and cynicism that has taken its place. It is business as usual in terms of the conflicts and violence with which the world still contends on a daily basis – with some new and terrifying realities. Major events such as the destruction of the Twin Towers in New York on 11 September 2001, the bombings in Madrid and London, the wars in Afghanistan and Iraq, and continuous conflict and displacement in Africa have brought yet more chaos and a deep sense of anxiety to the global community.

Our reaction to these events is paradoxical. Fear and distrust of 'the other' has once again taken centre stage, raising profound questions about 'national identity'. The revelations that two of the 21 July 2005 bombers had come to Britain as refugees when they were young children did not escape the tabloid headlines and leader writers, who used the opportunity to give fresh impetus to the ongoing anti-refugee campaign. This further reinforced the negative public discourse around asylum issues, revealing a deep vein of xenophobia and racism running through certain sectors of our society. But on the other hand, the British public's willingness not only to give generously but also to welcome survivors of crises into Britain has been an intermittent feature of public life as in, for example, the positive reception of Kosovan refugees in West Yorkshire in the spring of 1999 and that of Burmese refugees in

Sheffield in 2005; and the *Daily Mail*'s unprecedented criticism of the threatened deportation of Zimbabwean refugees in June 2005.¹ Time and again, when individual asylum seekers or their families are threatened with deportation, entire communities have been galvanised to defend their right to stay.²

But at a fundamental level, there is a perception that Britain's cultural and social landscape has changed beyond recognition, particularly since the terrorist attacks in London in July 2005. The unrestrained scapegoating of 'the other' in general and asylum seekers in particular echoes the anti-foreigner mindset against Jews, Chinese and Germans in the early years of the twentieth century.³ In the wake of the London bombings, racially motivated crime against Muslims rose by 500 per cent compared with the same period in the previous year, according to the Muslim Safety Forum.⁴

Being anti-asylum has now become a coded and socially acceptable form of racism legitimising racist attitudes in economic or cultural terms rather than in terms of race or colour.⁵ Many people do not differentiate between non-white people on the one hand and asylum seekers and other immigrants on the other. Nor do they make disctinctions between asylum seekers and other immigrants.⁶ It is not, however, just a question of colour: racism is also directed towards white Europeans from Eastern Europe, in particular Gypsies.⁷ The increase in Islamophobia since 9/11 may also be contributing to anti-asylum sentiment, and vice versa.⁸

As in the nineteenth and twentieth centuries, politicians today continue to make mileage out of the public's fears and insecurities. The conflation of asylum and immigration which surfaced in the 2005 pre-election period is only a slightly more sophisticated illustration of this time-dishonoured tradition.⁹ Both of the main parties vied with one another to appear 'tough' on these issues. The Conservative party slogan 'Are you thinking what we're thinking? – it's not racist to talk about immigration' was a way of signalling the idea that hostile feelings about 'others' were entirely acceptable.¹⁰ More explicitly, Bob Spink, the Tory candidate for Castle Point in

Essex, produced a leaflet saying: 'What part of "send them back" don't you understand, Mr Blair?'

Yet the anti-immigration and asylum platform failed to win any significant votes for the Conservatives. Meanwhile the Government's equivocation on the issue caused some disquiet within its own ranks. As one Labour MP pointed out after the election:

> The Government has never attempted to enunciate a clear set of principles that embrace the core concept of immigration – its associated economic and social dynamic, its role helping overcome structural productivity and pensions problems – or even embraced the psychology of the migrant when looking at school attainment, our general work ethic or patterns of benefit consumption. Instead the debate has moved rightwards.[11]

The overall refusal of both politicians and the press to deal with asylum and refugee issues in a transparent and open way is characteristic of how the issue has been treated for well over a hundred years. The hostile climate described throughout this book puts refugee and human rights organisations constantly on the defensive. Much of their energy is spent on reacting against this negative agenda instead of creating a positive one.

Can this anti-asylum tide be turned? If the goodwill shown by local campaigns and some sections of the local[12] and national press could be mobilised in more parts of the country, might it be possible to turn the asylum issue into a positive campaign along the lines of Jubilee 2000 and Make Poverty History? Could attitudes towards asylum be changed so that we no longer stigmatise the victim but put our energies into finding solutions? Could the system be made more manageable and less contentious, less emotive and less susceptible to the vagaries of both politicians and the press? Is it possible to create 'a small space in which to have a high quality debate among opinion formers and policy shapers about the future of the fundamental issues'?[13]

Even though there are no simple solutions, there is a great

deal that can be done to make the system better managed. Dispersed asylum seekers should not be placed in the most deprived and marginalised communities where they are perceived as a threat to public services; they should receive the same level of welfare benefits as British people and they should be allowed to support themselves by working while their applications are being processed.[14] This would accelerate the integration of those who win the right to remain in the UK and could facilitate the return of those who do not. Ironically, helping people integrate gives them the confidence to choose voluntary return where and when it is appropriate.

The reception, induction and support of refugees should be coordinated and organised so that people can ultimately regain control over their own lives. Self-sufficiency makes good economic sense. Forcing asylum seekers to be dependent by giving them inadequate financial support and prohibiting them from working sets up a cycle in which they become marginalized and unproductive.

The creation of a decision-making organisation independent of the Home Office, whose brief it is to investigate each asylum case on its own merits, could be a way of ameliorating some of the weaknesses of the present system. It would fast-track those whose cases are clear cut, and channel others according to the facts. This would save both time and resources and lead to better quality decisions.

In reshaping the asylum system, the notion of deterrence must give way to protection. This can only be done within a system which is not only better managed but also offers asylum seekers a fair hearing and treats them with dignity. In addition, the root causes of forced migration need to be addressed in more robust ways on the part of world leaders, too: the most effective way of reducing the number of asylum seekers is by reducing the number of people forced to flee their homelands in the first place. Preventing and resolving conflict and promoting respect for human rights and good governance worldwide – which includes stricter control on arms sales and a genuinely ethical foreign policy – should become priorities of governments everywhere.[15]

The UK government needs to revisit, rather than retreat from, the 1951 Refugee Convention. Inevitably, the world has changed since it was first introduced. But it is still a place where people need protection and a place of refuge. The 1951 Convention should still be the instrument that provides that protection. It is vital that the Convention is seen as sacrosanct, not only by the UK but by the European Union as a whole, so that responsibility for asylum seekers is shared and the case for protection becomes part of the moral framework for the entire European Union.

Even if the government introduced legislation that made the asylum system fairer, more efficient and transparent, public attitudes have become so entrenched that simply creating a better system in itself would do little to assuage the anxieties and fears of the general public. Myths are persistent and objective, non-partisan information is thin on the ground. Excellent resources that attempt to dispel myths about asylum seekers, such as *The Truth about Asylum*.[16] will reach only a limited audience. Schools offer some opportunity for looking dispassionately at asylum issues through their mandatory citizenship curriculum. But this too depends on the enthusiasm of teachers and the availability of good resources.

Part of the task of government is to set into place measures that can alter the public imagination so that, in the words of the journalist Yasmin Alibhai-Brown, we can be engaged in 'imaging the new Britain'.[17] This can only happen when the government shows its commitment to an ethical foreign and domestic policy.

At present asylum seekers do not have a real place in the government's strategy for ending social exclusion and increasing social cohesion and diversity. Refugee issues need to become part and parcel of social policy, and they have the potential for becoming just that, through the existing instruments of human rights legislation and the new Equalities Commission. If, as the Institute for Public Policy Research report suggests, politicians play the most significant role in the fostering of attitudes towards asylum seekers, then a more robust defence of the human rights of people to seek asylum could radically alter the way civil society engages with these issues.

By putting an end to the dehumanisation and negative rhetoric that presently envelops the asylum debate, we all stand to gain: those fleeing persecution will receive the protection they need and the abatement of suffering that this brings. And the rest of society will reap the benefits of reclaiming the humanity underpinning Britain's national narrative.

NOTES

1   Although sympathetic to the plight of Zimbabwean refugees, this article is used to criticise other asylum seekers and refugees in Britain, referring to the 'tens of thousands would-be refugees'. 'Don't Zimbabweans Have Human Rights', *Daily Mail*, 27 June 2005.

2   The deportation of the Thaha family in Plymouth is one such example. See http://www.ncadc.org.uk/archives/filed%20newszines/oldnewszines/news zine56/thaha.html.

3   Robert Winder, *Bloody Foreigners – The Story of Immigration to Britain*, (Little, Brown 2004), pp. 195–210.

4   Vikram Dodd,' Islamophobia blamed for attack', *Guardian*, (13 July 2005).

5   'Asylum: Understanding Public Attitudes', Miranda Lewis, Institute for Public Policy Research, 2005.

6   Ibid.

7   Ibid.

8   Ibid.

9   'Racist expressions towards asylum seekers appear to have become common currency and acceptable in a way which would never be tolerated towards any other minority.' *Guide to Meeting the Policing Needs of Asylum Seekers and Refugees*, London: Association of Chief Police Officers (ibid., see Chapter 7).

10 Conservative Party poster campaign (February–March 2005).

11 Jon Cruddas, MP, 'The long march against the BNP', *Guardian*, 20 May 2005.

12 A good illustration of appropriate local and national press coverage was seen in the way the *Guardian* (17 May 2005), the *Yorkshire Post* (17 May 2005) and the *Sheffield Star* (16 May 2005) reported on the Gateway programme run by

the United Nations High Commission for Refugees, a scheme established to resettle tens of thousands of refugees in the United States, Canada, Australia as well as the United Kingdom.

13   Maeve Sherlock, Chief Executive, Refugee Council in her foreword to *Refugees: Renewing the Vision. An NGO Workpaper on Improving the Asylum System* (London, Refugee Council, 2004).

14   Ibid.

15   Ibid., p. 10.

16   'Tell it like it is: The Truth About Asylum', Refugee Council, June 2006.

17   Yasmin Alibhai-Brown, *Who Do We Think We Are? – Imagining the New Britain*, (London, Penguin Books, 2000).

GLOSSARY OF TERMS

ASYLUM SEEKERS

In UK law these are people who say they have fled persecution, have applied for protection in another country and are awaiting a decision on their application.

The UN calls asylum seekers people who flee their own country for protection who may not fulfil the very narrow definition of refugee set out in the 1951 Convention.

DEPORTATION ORDER

Issued to asylum applicants after their claim and subsequent appeal has been rejected by the Home Office. Immigration officers have the power to detain those under an order until they are removed.

ECONOMIC MIGRANT

A person who leaves their own country to live in another in order to improve their standard of living and who is free to return to their own country whenever they wish.

HUMANITARIAN PROTECTION AND DISCRETIONARY LEAVE

These two new categories replaced *Exceptional Leave to Remain* in April 2003. They are designed for those whose applications for asylum have been refused but who can 'demonstrate they have protection needs' as laid out in the 1951 Convention. Asylum seekers are granted a period of up to three years to stay in the UK, after which they can apply for an extension or for permission to settle here permanently.

ILLEGAL ENTRANT

The 1951 Convention says that illegal entrants whose lives are in danger or who fear persecution should not be penalised, given that many regimes do not allow nationals to possess passports or travel documents.

ILLEGAL IMMIGRANT

A term created by the press and media that does not exist in law.

IMMIGRANT

A person who leaves their country voluntarily to live permanently in another.

IMMIGRATION AND NATIONALITY DIRECTORATE (IND)

The UK Home Office department responsible for immigration control at UK ports and airports and for assessing and processing asylum applications.

INDEFINITE LEAVE TO REMAIN

Permission given by the British government for asylum seekers to permanently settle in the UK.

REFUGEES

The United Nations ('Geneva') Convention Relating to the Status of Refugees was adopted in December 1951, following a resolution of the UN General Assembly in 1950, and came into effect in April 1954.

It defines a refugee as a person:

> [who] owing to [a] well-founded fear of being persecuted for reasons of race, religion, nationality, membership of a particular social group or political opinion, is outside the country of his nationality and is unable or, owing to such fear, is unwilling to avail himself of the protection of that country.

The 'well-founded fear of persecution' initially had to arise from events associated with the Second World War in Europe. The 1967 Protocol extended coverage to refugees throughout the world.

Obligations under the Convention fall squarely onto the receiving state and come into effect after the asylum seeker has entered its territory and made a claim for refugee status. The most basic principle, or core obligation, of signatory states is that of *non-refoulement*, i.e. not sending someone back to a situation where they might face persecution. Another important obligation (and source of increasing tension with the rise of people smuggling) is not to penalise asylum seekers for entering a signatory country 'illegally'.

While not spelled out as a requirement in the Convention, Western signatory states have, under the guidance of the UNHCR, established processes for determining asylum applications. Administrative and legal systems vary, but the central features are the same. Claims are assessed, on an individual basis, according to whether there is a 'real' possibility the claimant would face persecution if returned. Decisions are made on the basis of the credibility of the story, assisted by 'country information' gleaned from such sources as foreign affairs officials, Amnesty International and the US Department of State.

REGIONAL PROTECTION ZONES AND TRANSIT PROCESSING ZONES

These are UK proposals to European Union leaders that would set up protection zones and asylum application centres near the areas of conflict or countries from which large numbers of asylum seekers are fleeing. The idea is to prevent people crossing continents to seek asylum, often illegally, and to facilitate their return to their home countries once the conflict/crisis has passed. While the EU has rejected these proposals, the UK plans to set up a pilot project, likely to be in Kenya for Somali refugees.

SAFE THIRD COUNTRY RULE

An asylum claim can be rejected if the applicant can be returned to a listed safe third country, such as a country passed through by the asylum seeker on their way to the UK. There, the third country would assess their person's claim.

In addition, there is a *safe country list* composed of 24 countries considered 'safe' by the UK. Citizens of these countries are refused asylum by the Immigration and Nationality Directorate and their appeals will only be allowed outside the UK.

INDEX